Establish Your Foundation

L. A. Santana Jr.

Cadmus Publishing
www.cadmuspublishing.com

Copyright © 2022 L. A. Santana Jr.

Cover art by Francisco Moraga – fjmoragaproductions@gmail.com

Published by Cadmus Publishing
www.cadmuspublishing.com
Port Angeles, WA

ISBN: 978-1-63751-298-2
Library of Congress Control Number: 2022918629

All rights reserved. Copyright under Berne Copyright Convention, Universal Copyright Convention, and Pan-American Copyright Convention. No part of this book may be reproduced, stored in a retrieval system, or transmitted in any form, or by any means, electronic, mechanical, photocopying, recording or otherwise, without prior permission of the author.

Table of Contents

INTRODUCTION 1
HELL 6
SALVATION 15
REPENTENCE. 23
FAITH. 30
HOPE 39
GRACE 47
TRUTH 60
PRAYER. 66
FORGIVENESS 78
LOVE 89
FINAL CHAPTER 101
DEDICATIONS .109
ABOUT THE AUTHOR 111

INTRODUCTION

What is the purpose of a foundation? A foundation is meant to support whatever stands on it. It becomes the actual basis upon which that thing stands or is supported, (see Merriam Webster Dictionary and Thesaurus). A house relies upon a solid foundation to keep it standing. It does not depend solely on the material used to build that house because regardless of how good and valuable that material is, without a reliable foundation to help it stand, a strong enough wind, storm, or quake can bring it down to destruction. Whoa to those who rely upon the protection of that house. Great will be their fall.

Within my journey and growth in faith, I have come to understand the importance of establishing a firm foundation in everyone's life. I have realized that we, as human beings, are very much like houses and rely upon a foundation to stand. We have to face the struggles, hardships, trials, tribulations, and especially, the temptations of life. However, how we confront them can determine the fate of our future. If we respond to them in the wrong manner, it can cause us to fall, and that fall can be very destructive.

So many of us who place our faith in Jesus Christ have failed to remain standing when the storms of life come to us unexpected. The storms catch us off guard or unprepared and cause us to fall harder than others. This is because of what we rely on to keep us standing, and by standing, I mean standing in faith. We can't keep storms from coming. We can't stop trials, temptations, hardships, difficulties, or other kinds of suffering. These things will come at us in abundance.

What we can prevent is the outcome of facing these issues of life. The things we rely on to guide our response to them will determine if we remain standing at the end of it all. I had to learn this by trial and error, as we all do. I experienced a lot of failure, upsets, and disappointments when it came to the tests and temptations of life. I always responded to them in my own wisdom and understanding of things. Whenever I was confronted by one, I responded immediately, acting as if I knew how to resolve things without God's help.

In other words, I relied upon myself instead of my Lord and Savior Jesus Christ to see me through it all. This is why I fell so many times. I claim to have faith in Him, but when these tests came at me, I expressed to Him that I did not have faith in Him. I fell so many times that I finally had to examine myself and face the Truth. I had to answer the tough question, "do you really have faith?" The truth was yes, I had faith…in myself. This was why I kept on falling in my faith.

When things go well, I am full of faith and praise toward God, but when they got difficult and impossible, I had not faith at all. I tried everything I could to fix things my own way, and if I could not fix it, It would destroy me in some way. It was like the disciples in the boat with Jesus. I have faith in Him when He makes me to walk on water, but when the storms get loud, I begin to question His ability to keep me standing above water and prevent me from drowning. Although He tells me that He will not allow anything to hurt me because He is with me, when the storm rocks my boat, I fear dying and respond to it in my own strength instead of trusting Him.

Do you see what I mean? My house could not endure any storms. The storms revealed how weak and unreliable my foundation was. Jesus revealed to me that I had to establish my foundation if I expected to stand in the midst of the storm. I was guided by His Spirit to reflect upon all Jesus has accomplished for me, saw me through, and given me. I was reminded that He:

Delivered me from Hell
Allowed me to repent of my past lifestyle
Initiated my Faith
Gave me Hope
Gave me access to Grace unlimited
Gave me the Truth
Opened up a prayer line between Him, the Father, and me
Forgives me
Loves me; and
Has given me the gift of Salvation

These truths have reminded me of how much I am valued and loved by the One who encourages me to trust in Him with my life. This is what a house is doing when it is placed on top of a foundation; it is trusting its entire existence to the rock holding it up. Thus, my Savior asked that I trust in Him to be my foundation.

The question I asked myself was why not? Why am I not trusting Him? Why can I not trust the One who did all of this to save me from perishing?

The more I came to understand what He did for me and why He did these things for me, the more I was able to let go and trust in Him. These principles are the foundation I stand on today. It is a foundation that has allowed me to remain standing firm in faith no matter the circumstance and situation. The entire foundation pointed to Jesus, letting me know that there is no other foundation that can make me stand except the One my heavenly Father has laid down in my life.

This foundation has allowed me to endure the hardest times and seasons in my life and remain standing in faith. It has allowed me to grow in my relationship with God and in spiritual maturity day by day. Jesus did not promise those who believe in Him a life on earth free of suffering. He promised us a life full of love, joy, peace, patience, kindness, goodness, faith, gentleness, and self-control regardless of the hardships, difficulties, trials, tribulations, and temptations we may have to endure and overcome.

My hope for all of my readers is that these same principles serve as a firm foundation that can help you stand in faith during the hardest times of your life. I pray that when you are facing the storms of life, you are encouraged to reflect back on all of these things that Christ has accomplished for you, seen you through, and has given you, so that you understand how much He values and loves you.

The One who loves you will see you through anything life hands us. He will strengthen your weak parts and see through the work that He has begun in you until it is finished. All you need to do is establish yourself a firm foundation that will keep you standing in that faith.

I am not encouraging anyone to lay down any other foundation except for the One that has already been laid down in your life. That is Jesus Christ, our Lord and Savior. He alone has:

Delivered me from Hell
Allowed me to repent
Given me the gift of Salvation
Initiated my Faith
Given me Hope
Given me access to Grace
Given me the Truth
Opened a line for me of prayer
He grants me Forgiveness and
He has Loved me

What I offer you is a better understanding of these vital principles, to help you stand in times of trials and tribulations. By understanding what these principles mean, you can better understand what Jesus Christ has done for you out of His great love for you and use them as a foundation to stand on when faced with your storms of life.

May the Lord bless you as He has blessed me and He helps you stand in Faith. Enjoy.

Chapter 1

HELL

Have you ever heard someone say, "To hell with it," or, "to hell with him?" How about, "hell yeah," or, "hell no," or, "what the hell," or, "it's hot as hell?" The truth is that many people today do not take the subject matter on hell seriously because to them, hell is not real. Consequently, they end up finding out in the worst way…when they die.

Although, to many, hell is not considered a real place or something to take seriously. It was in the days of old when God, through prophets and the disciples, encouraged sinners to repent and place their faith in Jesus Christ for salvation. Repentance was encouraged to save those who are hell bound, due to the penalty of their sins.[1]

God hoped that people would understand that hell is very real and very serious. This is how serious it was to Him: 1.) He sent His Son, Jesus Christ, to earth; 2.) Jesus Christ left His

---

[1] John 3:3-7

position in heaven and became a man[2]; 3.) Jesus did this to fulfill God's requirements of righteousness for us, by living a holy, perfect, and faithful life (in thought, word, deed, and desire) towards God as a human being; 4.) After accomplishing this, Jesus gave His life as a sin offering, meaning that He had to suffer the penalty of sinning against a holy, just, and righteous God. The penalty was separation from God, death, and hell. Jesus suffered an excruciating death on the cross, was buried, and resurrected three days later; 5.) Although Jesus never committed sin Himself, God made Him sin for us so that we could become His righteousness. This means that He would take upon Himself the penalty of man's sins, so that all who have been cursed to death and hell (due to sin) can be saved and escape such a horrific penalty.[3] God did this because He understood how real and serious hell is.

Jesus did this for all who wish to escape the penalty of sinning against a holy, righteous, and just God who hates sin and evil.[4] He warned all sinners that if they repented of their sinful ways and lifestyle and placed their trust (faith/believe) in His finished works for salvation, they would not suffer the penalty of their sins. However, if they chose not to repent or trust in Him and His finished works for salvation, they will perish, because they chose to reject their only escape from the wrath of God.[5] He did this because hell is very real and serious. With that said, I will begin this lesson with an explanation of Hell.

---

[2] Isaiah 7:14;Matthew 1:18-23
[3] Matthew 26-28
[4] 2 Corinthians 5:21
[5] John 3:16-21;8:24;11:25-26;12:44-48

What is Hell?

There are three levels of hell that I would like to inform you on. In the Bible, they are known as Sheol, Hades, and Gehenna. All three of these are translated in the Bible as hell because of what they represent, however, it is of the utmost importance that every believer understands the difference and what each one represents.

<u>Sheol</u> is the Hebrew word used in the Old Testament that refers to the "pit," or, "grave." *Jacob* mentions going down into it to meet his dead son that laid in a grave; *Hannah* mentions that God is able to bring some to their death and send them to the grave; *Job* and *Isaiah* describe it as the place our dead bodies lay covered with dust and worms; and *Ezekiel* confirmed that this is the grave, pit, and burial place the dead are laid in.[6]

<u>Hades</u> is a Greek word used in the New Testament meaning dark, obscure, or the place of the departed spirits of the lost. It is a place of torment for the wicked. Jesus used this parable as a literal example of what the unsaved can expect after death and Sheol (the grave). Jesus specifically warned that the soul of the unsaved will be sent to Hades, where there will be suffering for that soul although it is absent from its body. The saved, however, will be comforted, at peace, and in paradise awaiting the Lord's return. This is a picture of what will happen to all the saved and unsaved souls after Sheol.[7]

<u>Gehenna</u> is the Hebrew name for a place known as the "Valley of Hinnom." This place became the place of pagan

---

[6] Genesis 37:35;1 Samuel 2:6; Job 21:13,23,26;24:19-20; Isaiah 14:9-11;38:9-10; Ezekiel 32:21-27

[7] Luke 16:19-31; Matthew 8:12, 11:23

worship and human sacrifices. Ahaz and Manasseh made their children, "pass through the fire," to Molech in this valley. Furthermore, this place was also known as the place the Jews used to burn dead corpses of animals and criminals. [8] In the New Testament, Gehenna is presented as the final punishment where the wicked are cast after the final judgement. It is the place where the body and soul of those in Hades are reunited and placed for eternity. It is described as a place of torment. Those condemned to Gehenna are not going to be exterminated. They will be transformed into an eternal state of being, where they will be made to suffer pain and punishment for eternity. Gehenna is made of fire that is unquenchable. It is a furnace and a lake of fire. It is outer darkness.[9]

Sheol is the first stop the saved and unsaved will go until the day of their physical resurrection. Once the soul departs from the body, the saved will go to paradise while the unsaved will immediately enter **Hades**.[10] The souls of the unsaved will be made to suffer until the final judgement. **Gehenna** is eternal judgement. It is where the body and soul of the unsaved will be united and made to suffer excruciating pain and torture for eternity. It will be the final stop for all who have rejected Jesus Christ as Lord and Savior.

Hell is eternal separation from God.[11] This means that the body and soul going there will be cut off from every good thing for eternity. The unrighteous, ungodly, and unrepented

---

[8] Joshua 15:8; Nehemiah 11:30; 1 Kings 16:3; 2 Kings 21:6; 2 Chronicles 28:3, 33:16; Isaiah 66:24; Daniel 12:2
[9] Matthew 5:22,29, 8:12, 13:42, 50, 18:9, 22:13, 25:30; Mark 9:45, 48; Revelation 19,20,20:10-15, 21:8
[10] Luke 23:43
[11] 2 Thessalonians 1:7-9

sinners are sentenced to this place.[12] God has sentenced all who have willfully rejected and refused to trust in Jesus Christ for salvation there because He has found all of mankind to be unrighteous and ungodly due to their natural instinct to sin against Him. Accordingly, He has declared that the penalty of sin is death and hell.[13]

Hell is Real

Hell is a real place where the lost shall suffer for eternity. The story Jesus gives of the rich man and Lazarus is true, not just a figurative example as some would have us believe. Jesus informed us that when the rich man died, he went to hell (Hades) where apparently, the rich man suffered. Jesus also warned that we should fear God because He can destroy both the body and the soul in hell (Gehenna), which indicates that hell is a literal place because our physical bodies cannot be cast into some metaphorical place. This leads to our next point about hell. What is it like?

What is Hell like?

In the story of the rich man and Lazarus, Jesus informed us that when the rich man died and went to hell, the rich man was in torment. He was begging for mercy and severely dehydrated, seeking a drop of water to cool off his burning tongue. The rich man was inflamed…burning! Just to help you understand what this man was experiencing, understand that to be

---

[12] Holman Illustrated Dictionary, Romans 1:18-32; 1 Corinthians 6:9-10
[13] Genesis 2:16-17;Romans 3:9-18,23,5:6-10,6:3-10,23

in torment is to experience a combination of *great* mental anguish, harassment, and displeasure. The level of torment this man was experiencing in hell (Hades), although we know it was not physical because he was not united with his body, is incomparable to any we can ever experience on earth.

The prophet Isaiah described hell as a place of torment where the fire is never put out.[14] Jesus Christ described it as a place of destruction. He said it was a lake of fire where the fire was unquenchable. He said it was a fiery furnace where those who were sent there would be weeping and gnashing their teeth. Jesus said it was outer darkness.

The people who are cursed to eternity in hell are made to suffer so much because hell is eternal separation from God. God is the source of everything that is good. To be cut off from God is to be cut off from everything that is good. On the Day of Judgment, everyone will be given a body that will never die. The book of Revelation speaks to this point. Now imagine experiencing everything the rich man experienced and having an eternal body, cut off from God and everything that is good, where all you will have to experience is physical pain and torture. This means that all you will experience in hell is not good.

There are people alive today who, by the grace of God, have experienced hell so that they can share their testimony with those God desires to save. Bill Wiese is one of the few Christians that God has allowed to experience hell, so that the world may know that it is real. It is the worst place to end up

---

[14] Isaiah 50:11, 60:24

in, and it is somewhere a loving God would allow the person who rejects His gift (Jesus Christ) of salvation to go.[15]

In his book, Bill explained that there will be demons waiting to torture you in hell. They will hate you as they hate God because you were created in His image and likeness. Every time they look at you, they will see God, so their hate for God will be expressed towards you. You will not be able to escape them. They are huge, strong, and ugly. They will break every bone in your body, and you will feel every ounce of pain without the option of escaping or retreating somewhere. They will torture you. In addition, you will feel the scorching heat burning you internally and externally, but you will not die because you are already dead.

CONCLUSION

Hell is three-fold:

Sheol (the grave)

Hades (where the soul goes immediately and suffers after death).

Gehenna (Final stop, where the body and soul are reunited to suffer eternal punishment).

God is Love. It is not His desire that any perish in hell. God gave His only begotten Son (Jesus Christ) to die for the sins of the world, so that whoever trust/relies/depends in His finished works for salvation, would never perish in hell, but have eternal life after death.[16] That was His ultimate act of Love. If

---

[15] 23 MINUTES IN HELL by Bill Wiese
[16] John 3:16

you reject His gift, you are rejecting His attempt to rescue you from hell.

Therefore, if you end up in hell, it is not because a loving God sent you there. It is because you chose to suffer the penalty for your sins.

Hell is real! Hell is serious! Hell is no joke! Is it Heaven or Hell? For all who have chosen heaven, by trusting in Jesus Christ for salvation, do not forget this precious gift. Tell your parents, children, friends, or enemies about the gift of God. Be the one God can use to save their souls from Hell.

Q & A on HELL

1. What are the 3 levels of hell according to the author's writing?
2. What keeps you out of hell?
3. What are the descriptions of hell according to the Bible?
4. What is the purpose of hell?
5. What is the difference between hell & the lake of fire? (Read Revelation Chapter 19+20).
6. How serious does God take hell?
7. Before reading about hell, what did you think it was? Where did you think you would go after you die?

_____

_____

_____

Chapter 2

SALVATION

There are many Christians in the world today who, if asked, "what does it mean to have the gift of salvation," cannot answer the question for a lack of knowledge and understanding on the subject. This lack of knowledge and understanding has resulted in many failing to: 1.) Come to true repentance; 2.) Intimately know Jesus Christ; 3.) Learn how-to walk-in faith; 4.) Develop into a mature Christian; 5.) Grow in the grace of God; 6.) Grow in prayer; and 7.) Fulfill God's commandments.

In this second chapter, I'll explain the true meaning of salvation for anyone who does not know or understand it. My goal in this explanation is to help everyone seeking salvation to understand the gift they are receiving and what they can expect out of their salvation. However, to understand salvation, we must understand why we need it in the first place. Therefore, I begin this lesson with an explanation on why we need salvation.

WHY DO WE NEED SALVATION?

The Bible teaches us that God has looked down from heaven to earth seeking a righteous person and declared that He has found no one on Earth that met His standard for righteousness.[17] He has declared that all of mankind has sinned and fallen short of His glory.[18] Being that God has found no man, woman, or child on earth that is righteous, this means that no matter how much good we do or how hard we try to appear righteous before God, escape hell, and make it to heaven on our own efforts, we will always fall short due to our corrupted state of being and sinful imperfections. We will always, *"miss the mark,"* when trying to appear righteous before Him, escape hell, and make it into heaven by our own efforts because He has already judged us according to our imperfections, weaknesses, faults, errors, and overall sinful nature.

To sin means to disobey God and/or rebel against Him. This means to, "miss the mark," or, "target" God has required us to hit for righteousness. Many try to do good, believing that they can earn righteousness, escape hell, and make it into heaven, but because we can never hit the target required to obtain these things, we would never be able to earn it. This is why God declared we, "are all as an unclean thing, and all our righteousness are as filthy rags." [19] He needs us to understand this very important fact because it is the main reason we need Him and salvation. He is the only one who can provide us with righteousness, deliverance from hell, and access into heaven,

---

[17] Psalms 14:1-4;Romans 3:10-18
[18] Romans 3:23
[19] Isaiah 64:6

through the forgiveness of our sins and death/resurrection of Jesus Christ.

Without salvation, we will suffer in Hell for eternity. Without it, we will be tormented and made to suffer for eternity because our sinful ways and deeds have earned our way to Hell. As it is written, "The wage of sin is death; but the gift of God is eternal life through Jesus Christ."[20] It is for this reason that God gave His only begotten Son. Whoever believes (trust/relies/depends) on His finished works for salvation will never perish but receive eternal life.[21] Jesus Christ is the gift of God for anyone who desires to be *saved* from the penalty of their sins and delivered from its lifestyle. Without His gift for salvation there will be no escape. This is why we need salvation. This brings us the next topic of discussion. What is salvation?

WHAT IS SALVATION?

Salvation is the *deliverance* from the power or penalty of sin. According to the Holman Illustrated Bible Dictionary, this means that we have been forgiven as sinners and released from sin. This required Christ's sacrifice as punishment of sin. Our sin has been put away and we have been delivered from the power of sin until redemption of the body.[22] It is also described as the act of *redemption.*

Redemption means to let someone go free for a ransom. It is the recalling of captives (sinners) from captivity (sin) through the payment of ransom (Christ's death). Sin is slavery

---

[20] Romans 6:23
[21] John 3:16
[22] Matthew 26:28;Luke 1:77;Romans 7:24-25, 8:23, 2 Corinthians 1:9-10; Ephesians 1:6-7; Hebrews 9:22, 10:18

and sinners are its slaves.[23] Jesus paid the *ransom* (price) for redeeming captives, releasing them from their bonds and setting them free.[24]

Now that you know what salvation is, we now want to get into the fruit of salvation. We want you to know the gift of salvation, which is important for Christian growth, development, and maturity.

WHAT DOES SALVATION PROVIDE?

Sin is disobedience or rebellion toward God, which has placed a curse upon everyone who lives in it or practice it.[25] Today many are suffering as a direct result of their rebellion and disobedience. They have placed themselves in danger or harm's way by living in sin.

All who have disobeyed God, by breaking His commands, are guilty of breaking them all.[26] Since we have all broken one or more of His commands, we have all been found guilty and sentenced to death and everlasting punishment in hell. However, anyone who has received God's gift of salvation by trusting in Jesus Christ as their Lord and Savior, has been redeemed and delivered from the penalty of sin. This means that they are no longer having to worry about going to hell.

Therefore, the *first* thing that salvation provides is deliverance from the penalty of sin, which is death and hell, (John 3:16).

---

[23] John 8:34; Romans 6:17, 20; 2 Peter 2:19
[24] Matthew 20:28; 1 Timothy 2:6
[25] Deuteronomy 28
[26] James 2:10

Secondly, when God created man and woman, He created us in His image and likeness, which means that they were to Him like looking into a mirror.[27] Every time He looked upon us, He saw His own reflection. As His representatives, everyone in the world saw Him in us when they looked upon us. This means that we were morally pure, righteous, holy, wise, and perfect like our Creator. He created us in a manner where, through us, He can rule and allow others to get to know Him. In this state of being, we were able to bring Him glory because we were spiritually one with Him.

However, when we decided to be disobedient towards Him, we died spiritually, and our godly nature was corrupted. Our ability to glorify Him departed. We became the opposite of what He created us to be. Instead of His representatives, we became representatives of darkness, evil, destruction, and death, which means that He can no longer rule through us.

Nevertheless, all who have received the gift of salvation has been made spiritually alive again. This means we have been born-again of God and given a living spirit (new life) that is united with our God.

Therefore, the *second* thing salvation provides us with is new life. God raised us from death to life with Jesus Christ. He caused us to be born-again of Him, adopting us as His children, and brought us back to our original state, so that we can be one with Him again, represent Him, and rule as He intended. Now we are able to bring Him glory again.

Finally, sin has separated us from God because He is pure and holy, so He cannot be around sin. In fact, God hates sin, which made us His enemies as long as our sin remained un-

---

[27] Genesis 1:26

paid for. Consequently, He does not hear the prayers of His enemies, because this can only be enjoyed if we are in a right relationship with Him. To have our prayers heard, we must be able to enter His presence.

Since God is Spirit, we can only enter His presence spiritually. Thus, we must be made spiritually alive again and spiritually one with Him. Sin made us spiritually dead and cut us off from Him. Although He is still merciful to those who are cut off from Him, by giving them the abilities to enjoy another day of life, breadth, sight, hearing, taste, good health, and other things that are taken for granted, this is not because they asked Him for it. This is simply because His love provides us with what we need with the hope that we will eventually be saved from the penalty of our sins.

Only a child of God can enjoy His presence, have their prayers heard, and receive His grace. Until the sin in our lives is paid for and forgiven, none will be able to enjoy this type of relationship with Him. Those who have accepted the blood sacrifice of Jesus Christ need only to confess daily sins to remain in unbroken fellowship with Him.[28] It is for this reason that we are able to come to His throne (the holy of holies), enter His presence, communicate with Him (prayer), and obtain grace and mercy in our time of need.[29]

Therefore, the *third* thing salvation provides us with is a right relationship with God. It restores our relationship with Him, which allows our prayers to be heard and unlimited access to His grace in our time of need, (1 Corinthians 1:9).

---

[28] 1 John 1:9
[29] Ephesians 2:11-19; 2 Corinthians 5:18-21; Hebrews 4:16; 1 John 1:9-10

CONCLUSION

Therefore Salvation:

Delivers us from the penalty of sin which is destruction, death, and hell.

Gives us new life (Born-Again as a Child of God).

Restores our relationship with God (Prayers are heard/received and grace is made available).

All of this is accomplished through faith and grace in Jesus Christ our Lord and Savior!

Q & A on SALVATION

1. What are the 7 steps when you have true knowledge and understand to obtain salvation?
2. What does it mean to sin? How have you missed the mark God wants?
3. What does salvation provide for the sinner? What does salvation provide for the saved?
4. When did sin first come into the world? Who and what does sin effect?
5. When we receive salvation, what comes with it? If we reject salvation, what comes with it?
6. What does it mean to be spiritually alive?
7. How does Jesus Christ's sacrifice compare to the Old Testament sacrifices?

_____

_____

_____

Chapter 3

REPENTENCE

Many desire to be saved from the penalty of sin, which is darkness, destruction, death, and hell. Unfortunately, they fail to understand that without repentance and faith in Jesus Christ they cannot be saved. Repentance is so essential for salvation that God gave this ministry to Jesus Christ, John the Baptist, the disciples, and His Church. The ministry of repentance was meant to prepare people for salvation by encouraging them to turn from their sinful ways and place their faith in Jesus Christ.[30] However, today, even if they desired to repent, they wouldn't know how because they don't understand what it means to repent or why it's necessary for salvation. Therefore, I begin this lesson by answering the first question. What does it mean to repent?

---

[30] Matthew 28:18-20; Mark 16:15-16; Luke 24:47

WHAT DOES IT MEAN TO REPENT?

Biblically, repentance means that one has had a change of mind towards sin, regrets giving into it, and is remorseful because of it. This attitude ultimately leads to a turning away from it. Your change of mind, regret, remorse, and turning away comes from learning and experiencing the truth about sin, its consequences, and penalties.[31] Without this truth, there would be no reason to repent.

Many do not realize that a sin committed against themselves (lust of the flesh, lust of the eyes, or pride of life) or other people is a sin committed against God. Once it is understood that our sin, no matter who it is directed towards, is against God and He has declared that the consequence of sinning leads one into darkness, destruction, death, and hell, one should be encouraged to repent. This change of mind, regret and remorse towards sin is needed to awaken all men to their desperate need for God's saving grace (salvation). This is the truth about sin and what leads an individual to make the decision to turn away from a sinful lifestyle and receive Jesus Christ as their Lord and Savior.

Therefore, the meaning of repentance is a change of mind, regret, remorse, and turning from a sinful lifestyle to Jesus Christ for deliverance from the control of sin and its penalty.

WHY DO WE NEED TO REPENT?

Our sinful ways and nature have brought enmity between us and God. Enmity is hatred, the kind that is felt for an en-

---

[31] Holman Illustrated Bible Dictionary

emy, which means that God, who is the only one able to save us from the penalty of our sins, provide for our needs, and protect us from evil hates sin so much that He regards anyone who makes a practice of sin His enemy. Thus, anyone who has not had their sins paid for with the blood of Christ remains under God's judgement and is cursed to darkness, destruction, death, and hell.

As mentioned in the previous chapter, God has declared that "All have sinned and fallen short of the glory of God," and "the wage of sin is death."[32] His word says, "Know ye not that the unrighteous shall not inherit the Kingdom of God? Be not deceived: neither fornicators, nor idolaters, nor adulterers, nor effeminate, nor abusers of themselves with mankind, nor thieves, nor covetous, nor drunkards, nor revilers, nor extortioners, shall inherit the Kingdom of God."[33]

His point is that there is not one person on earth that He does not consider a sinner, an enemy, and condemned. With that knowledge, He wants us to know that there is no exception. If you are a sinner, you will not make it into heaven.

However, God has made a way for all who are under the curse of sin to reverse it through acceptance of Jesus Christ's righteousness and death on the cross. He desires that none perish, but that all of mankind obtains eternal life. To perish does not mean that we will cease to exist. It means to change from your original form and nature to something else. This is important to understand because nothing that exists can ever cease to exist. It only becomes something else in form and nature.

---

[32] Romans 3:23,6:23; Exodus 20:1-17; Matthew 5:17-48
[33] 1 Corinthians 6:9-10; Galatians 5:19-21; Ephesians 5:5

God does not desire that we cease to exist in the form and nature He created us to be. However, sin has corrupted and deformed us. Thus, we are already perishing without Christ in our lives.

God desires to deliver us from darkness, destruction, death, and hell. He desires to transform us from His enemies into His children and share an intimate relationship with us. If we are not willing to turn from this sinful lifestyle to Jesus Christ for salvation, the curse will remain, and we will suffer the consequences. It is that simple.

John the Baptist preached repentance from a sinful lifestyle because without repentance there is no salvation.[34] However, when the people heard him preach, many showed up to be baptized with the intent of being saved from the penalty of sin but were not willing to turn away from their sinful lifestyle. Realizing that this was the case, John sharply reprimanded them. He knew that they were seeking salvation without repenting, so he warned them to "Bring forth fruit worthy of repentance."

The fruit that he is talking about is change of mind towards sinning against God, regretting that we've sinned against Him, and feeling so remorseful that we are willing to turn away from it and demonstrate to God how much more we desire Him over sin. In other words, He was looking for a humble attitude in them that expressed sincere recognition of their sinful state and desperate need of saving. This form of repentance comes only when one realizes the true danger and harm that sin has placed them in with God.

Today, we have many claiming to believe in Jesus Christ because they believe this will help them to escape the penalty of

---

[34]   Matthew 3:2

sins, however, they do not desire to be delivered from their sinful lifestyle, but only from the penalty that comes with it. These are the same people that John had strictly warned to "bring forth fruit" that is "worthy of repentance."

CONCLUSION

God desires to save us from sin and its curses. His desire is to make us His children. He desires that we be in a right relationship with Him, but we must be delivered from sin and the lifestyle of sin that has separated us from Him. This is the opportunity repentance gives us. This is why Jesus gave His life on the cross for us, that through Him, all of our sins (past/present/future) have been paid for, we can obtain His righteousness, and become His children.

Repentance produces a change of mind, regret, remorse, and a turning away of sin. Repentance comes from learning the truth about sin, the consequences of sin, the penalty of sin, and a desire within to be saved and delivered from sin and its lifestyle. This then leads one to make the conscious decision to crucify their sinful nature (old self) and bury him/her with Jesus Christ, so that just as Jesus was raised from the dead in new life, you too may be resurrected into *new life* and become a child of God through the faith you place in Him for salvation.[35]

Therefore, repentance means:

One has changed their mind towards sinning against God.

One is full of regret due to giving in to sin because of its curses and consequences (separation from God).

---

[35] Romans 6:3-13

One has become remorseful and desires to be delivered from its penalty (sinful bondages, darkness, destruction, death, and hell).

One has decided to turn away from the sinful lifestyle that has brought this curse upon them and receive a new life in Christ Jesus.

Q & A on REPENTENCE

1. Why is repentance so important?
2. What does it mean to repent?
3. What will encourage one to repent?
4. Why do we need repentance?
5. What did John the Baptist mean when he said, "Bring forth fruit worthy of repentance"? (See Matthew 3:8).
6. What is the main thing about this lesson that will resonate with you the most?

_____

_____

_____

Chapter 4

FAITH

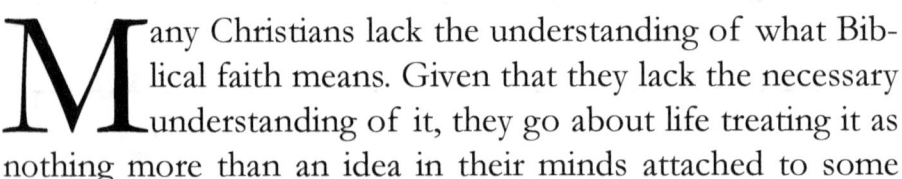

Many Christians lack the understanding of what Biblical faith means. Given that they lack the necessary understanding of it, they go about life treating it as nothing more than an idea in their minds attached to some feelings. This is why many lack the faith they need to be saved, grow in spiritual maturity, and grow in a relationship with God.

If most people were asked to explain what faith means to them, they could not explain it, but that does not mean that they do not know how to express it. The truth is that we all demonstrate faith in the people, places, and things we know, trust, believe in, rely on, and depend on. What we do not realize is that in order to express faith, we need an object to believe in, rely on or depend on in order to place our faith in it. When we realize this fact, we will begin to understand that the issues with faith are always dealing with the object of our faith.

Although time and experience reveal to us that the objects of our faith are faulty and unreliable, we still dedicate a great amount of faith in them because it is all we know. The Christian who fails to get to know the God who has created and saved them will also be inclined to place their faith in the only things they know, although nothing or no one is more reliable, trustworthy, and dependable than the Creator.

Failure to know and understand that God is the most reliable, trustworthy, and dependable object to place faith in will lead us to plant our faith in the unreliable. Thus, we will continually reap upsets, failures, and disappointments. For enlightenment on this matter, I begin this lesson with the meaning of faith.

THE MEANING OF FAITH

Dr. Tony Evans gave a great sermon on the *Concept of Faith* coming out of Hebrews 11:1. In his sermon, he says, "Faith is only as meaningful as the substance it is attached to. If you have faith in bad substance, then your faith will be insufficient no matter how much you possess. Your substance must be real and reliable. The surer the substance, the more solid the faith, because faith is directly related to the substance it is attached to. The bigger the substance, the bigger the faith."

Therefore, faith is *trust, reliance,* and *dependence* in substance one believes to be reliable, dependable, and trustworthy. In relation to God, faith is initiated in the believer as a response to who He reveals Himself to be, what He has said, and what He has done in the Old Testament (for the children of Israel) and the New Testament (through the person of Jesus Christ His

Son).[36] Therefore, when the Christian claims to have faith in God or Jesus Christ, they are claiming that they are confident He is unfailing, reliable, dependable, and trustworthy.

How reliable, dependable, or trustworthy the object of our faith is, will determine the value of our faith. In other words, if there is a chance that the substance of your faith can fail you, disappoint you, or let you down, your faith will lose value.

FAITH AND FEAR IN GOD

In the Old Testament, faith and fear in God is one in the same. To have faith in God meant that an individual relies on God, depends on God's unchanging character, and trusts in His faithfulness. This faith is based on who He has revealed himself to be because everything He has said, claimed, or promised has happened and/or will happen, our faith in Him is secure. This is because faith is based on what He has done in the past and present, which gives us confidence in what He will do in the future.

So, how does faith relate to fear? The knowledge and revelation we receive of God ignites a natural response of fear in us, towards Him, that comes by faith not terror or horror. When God reveals himself to be who He claims to be and does what He says He will do, the person experiencing His faithfulness naturally fears disobeying, displeasing, or dishonoring Him because He is true.

In other words, they will take Him serious and act like everything He says is true because He has proven Himself to be so. To take Him serious in character, word, and deed is to fear

---

[36] Holman Illustrated Bible Dictionary

Him. Fear in God, however, expresses faith in Him; and when we express faith in God fear comes naturally.[37]

FAITH IS THE SUBSTANCE OF HOPE AND EVIDENCE OF THE UNSEEN

God has always required that we have faith in Him for salvation.[38] He wants all to be forgiven and saved of their sins. He wants all to know Him and receive the gift of eternal life.[39] He wants all to become His children and spend eternity with Him in heaven.[40] He wants us to be blessed by Him.[41] However, without faith we cannot obtain anything from God. God has revealed Himself, spoken, and acted through Jesus Christ His Son. He did this so that He can draw all of humanity to Him. Unless we whole-heartedly and sincerely place our trust, reliance, and dependence in Jesus Christ, what He says, and what He has done for salvation we cannot be saved.[42]

His word says, "Without faith it is impossible to please Him. For he that comes to God must first believe that He is and that He is a rewarder of those who diligently seek Him," (Hebrews 11:6). Here, the Hebrew writer is warning all seeking to obtain anything from God that we should examine our hearts to make sure that it expresses no doubt that God is real or exists and that we truly believe that based on His word and faithfulness, He will do as He said He will do.

---

[37] Genesis 22:12; Hebrews 12:5-11
[38] Genesis 15:6; Deuteronomy 1:1-33; Habakkuk 2:4
[39] John 17:3
[40] John 1:12-13,3:3-5
[41] Ephesians 1:3,11-14
[42] John 3:16

This is what God is looking to find when we come to Him asking or expecting to receive from him. Although we may not receive it when we expect to, if we are sure about God, we will wait patiently for it because the One who we rely on to provide it is faithful and able. This is the kind of faith that is pleasing to Him.

His word states that, "Faith is the substance of things hoped for and the evidence of things not seen," (Hebrews 11:1). Let's look at it like this; Jesus Christ is the substance of our faith because, aside from being the Son of God, He has proven Himself to be trustworthy, reliable, and dependable. He has proven to be our Rock, the Way, Truth, Life, our good Shepherd, and our Redeemer.[43] We know that He is faithful and cannot lie.[44] He is All-Powerful.[45] Based on what we know about Him we know that there is no better substance to have faith in than Him.

Faith then, in Jesus, becomes the substance (the key) of the things we hope for (expect to receive or obtain). Our faith in Him becomes the evidence of things not seen. In other words, because He is the key for obtaining what I expect to obtain, when I use it (faith) I can obtain what I hope for (the unseen).

SAVING FAITH

Unless an individual *repents* of their sinful ways, calls upon Jesus Christ to save them from the penalty of their sins, and ask Him to be the Lord of their lives, they cannot be saved.[46]

---

[43] 1 Corinthians 10:4, John 10:11, 14:6, 16, 17
[44] 1 Corinthians 1:9; 1 Thessalonians 5:24; 2 Thessalonians 3:3; 1 John 1:9
[45] Matthew 28:18
[46] Romans 10:9-5

However, this requires confession (acknowledge/admit/declare) with the mouth that Jesus is the Lord (ruler) of our lives and belief (trust) in our hearts that God raised Him from the dead. In other words, this confession and belief is based on the knowledge and understanding of who Jesus is and what He has done for us.

The person confessing Jesus as Lord and believing in their heart that God raised Him from the dead understands that Jesus died for our sins, that God accepted His sacrificial death as an offering for our sins, that through Him we have forgiveness for our sins, in Him we have received righteousness, in Him, we have salvation, and through faith in Him, we obtain it all. This is saving faith.

WHY FAITH IN JESUS?

The word of God calls us to place our faith in Jesus Christ because He is the *way,* the *truth,* and the *life* and no one can come to the Father except they go through Him. Furthermore, He is responsible for all of creation. He is the Son of God, the Word of God, and the Bread of life. He is the Resurrection, the Good Shepherd, the Alpha and Omega, and the Beginning and the End.[47] Jesus is our salvation, peace, hope, strength, guidance, light, truth, joy, grace, mediator, and life.

God has revealed Himself, spoken, and acted through the person of Jesus Christ. Through Jesus, God has allowed us to know and experience Him. We are confident that He will never lie to us or fail us. Faith in Him is not an idea attached to some feeling. It is a way of life, which is manifested in and through

---

[47] Matthew 11:27; John 1:1, 1:1-3, 6:35, 10:11, 11:25; Revelation 22:13

the believer by his or her response to the word of Jesus. Jesus Christ is the Author and Finisher of our faith.[48] He is our Savior. Without Him, there is no life. This is why we ought to have faith in Him.

FAITH IS AN ACTION

In the book of James, we find a description of faith that seems different from how Paul describes faith to the Romans. For example, Paul says that Abraham was justified of God by faith in reference to Genesis 15:6. Specifically, he says that because Abraham believed God, God accredited his belief to him as righteousness. He makes clear that it wasn't by works that Abraham was justified. Later on, he explains that righteousness cannot be obtained through the observance of the law, but through faith.

James, however, explains that faith needs works because without it, it is dead. He says that Abraham was justified by works when He offered Isaac on the altar to God. He informs us that when he did this, his faith was working together with his works; therefore, his faith was made perfect by his works. Thus, when Scripture tells us that, "Abraham believed God, and it was accounted to him for righteousness."[49] James tells us that this means a man is justified by work and not solely by faith, concluding the faith without works in dead faith.[50]

So, how do we reconcile the two? First of all, it is important to understand that the two are not speaking of faith in

---

[48] Hebrew 12:2
[49] Genesis 15:6
[50] James 2:14-26

the same sense. When Paul speaks of faith, he associates it with righteousness. Therefore, he uses Abraham as an example of how one obtains righteousness. He highlights that God justified Abraham because Abraham believed Him. However, James associate's faith with works. Not to obtain righteousness but to represent what we claim to believe and who we believe in. Therefore, he uses Abraham as an expression of faith.

Christians are called to apply what God says to our feet. To put it another way, Tony Evans said that faith is acting like what God says is true. He also reconciled the two descriptions of faith we read about in the following sense: "Faith is acting like it is so, even when it's not so, in order that it might be so, simply because God said so." This means that faith is also an action.

CONCLUSION

Faith is:

Belief, trust, reliability, and dependency in who we know to be unfailing, true, faithful, trustworthy, reliable, and dependable.

Fear (respecting and taking God seriously).

The substance of things hoped for, and evidence of things not seen.

Faith is an action.

Q & A on FAITH

1. How do people demonstrate faith throughout their daily lives?
2. What do you need to express faith?
3. What is the meaning of faith?
4. How is faith initiated in the believer? (Explain in your own words).
5. How does fear in God relate to faith in God?
6. What does it mean to fear God?
7. What does the writer mean in Hebrews 11:1 when he said, "Faith is the substance of things hoped for and the evidence of things not seen"?
8. What is saving faith?
9. Why should we have faith in Jesus Christ?
10. Do you agree that faith is an action? If so, explain.

_____

_____

_____

Chapter 5

HOPE

In the previous lesson, we've learned that faith is the substance (key) of things hoped for (expect to receive or obtain), such as the riches in a safe that only a key can open. In other words, hope requires faith. What you expect to receive or obtain is accompanied with belief, trust, reliability, and dependency in the person we trust, rely on, and depend on to provide us with what we hope for.

We have learned that faith is the evidence of the things we cannot see, meaning that it produces or brings into reality what we do not or have not obtained yet.[51] That unseen thing is our hope. In this lesson, we will learn what hope means, what we should hope for, and why hope is important because too many Christians hope for the wrong things. They hope for what is physical. In other words, they hope for what their five senses can detect, but this is not hope.

---

[51] Hebrews 11:1

WHAT IS HOPE?

According to the Holman Illustrated Bible Dictionary, biblical hope is trustful expectation. Biblically, the Christian hope is the expectation of a favorable outcome under God's guidance. More specifically, Christian hope is the confidence that what God has done for us in the past guarantees our share in what God will do in the future. It is not to be confused with a feeling or wishful thinking. Biblical hope is a trustful expectation and desire of something from God, but it isn't tied to what pleases the flesh, which means that it is not based on physical things.

In Romans 8:24, the Apostle Paul says, "Hope that is seen is not hope, for what man seethe why doth he yet hope for?" Paul is referring to material things that Christians tend to hope for. The riches of the world, such as money, houses, cars, clothes, and other material things, are not things we need to hope for because they are already in the world. We can pray to God to help us obtain them, according to our need, but they should not be the things we hope for because we are not of this world. These are things we can obtain on our own through faith in God, hard work, responsibility, sacrifice, and wisdom. These are already in the world in great quantity, so why hope for them? God has already given them to us, so go and get it. We do not need to wait on God to provide it for us anymore.

The Christian that places their hope in the things of the world (the physical) is not focused but distracted.[52] We are not from the world; therefore, we do not belong here. It is important to come to terms with this reality because we will not

---

[52] Colossians 3:1-2

spend eternity here.[53] This is not where Christ our Lord will rule from. We are to look forward to a new heaven and a new earth that we have inherited in Christ Jesus.

While we remain in this world, we are to take advantage of the opportunity to build for ourselves riches in heaven because it is our ultimate goal to get there.[54] Paul said, "But if we hope for that we see not, then do we with patience wait for it," (Romans 8:25). In other words, we are to hope for what we cannot see, which are the actual promises of God (eternal unseen things). This is what we should be looking forward to. This is the hope of our faith. Thus, we wait to receive it with patience, knowing that we will obtain them when we are no longer on this earth.

Biblical hope is a strong and confident expectation of a future regarding what God has promised us.[55] Paul argued that hope was a basis of salvation for Christians, which means that the Christians should be focused on salvation. However, biblical hope is attached to the reality that you will receive what you hope for based on God's trustworthiness, reliability, and dependability. God is the object of our faith because we know that He is unfailing, true, faithful, all-knowing, all-powerful, and that He has proven Himself to be unchanging. He is the object of our hope. He gives us confidence that we can completely trust to receive all He says we will receive or obtain from Him.

---

[53] John 17:16
[54] Matthew 6:19-21
[55] Titus 1:2

WHAT SHOULD WE HOPE FOR?

Many Christians came into the faith hoping in vain, worthless, and useless things. Others do not know what to hope for, so they are hopeless. All those things God has promised us in Christ, which we have not yet received, except for part of our salvation (which has been given to us already), is what we should hope for.

Paul gave us a small preview of what we should hope for in Romans 8:17 when he mentions that we are "joint-heirs" with Christ. This is referring to the fact that we will be glorified together with Christ, being transferred from a corrupt body into an incorruptible one, (v.21). What a beautiful hope; the thought of not having to suffer pain, worry, stress, depression, addiction, sadness, oppression, and all the other evils that wear us down. This is the hope we look forward to when our Lord takes us with Him to heaven. Here is a list of the other things we can hope for in Christ:

Authority over the nations (Revelations 2:26).
Approval from God (Mark 8:38; Luke 9:26; 2 Timothy 4:8).
Beauty for ashes (Isaiah 61:3).
Becoming pillars in God's temple (Revelation 3:12).
Crown of life (James 1:12; Revelation 2:10, 4:10-11).
Crown of glory (1 Peters 5:1-4).
Crown of righteousness (2 Timothy 4:8).
Eat of the hidden manna (Revelation 2:17).
Incorruptible crown (1 Corinthians 9:25).
New Heaven and New Earth (Revelation 21:7).
Name inscribed in the book of life (Revelation 3:5).
Name confessed before the Father (Revelation 3:5).
Not hurt by the second judgement (Revelation 2:11).

Receiving a white stone and a new name (Revelation 2:17).

Receiving good things from the Lord Jesus (Ephesians 6:8).

Reward for good deeds (1 Corinthians 3:11-15).

Reigning forever (Daniel 7:18-28; Matthew 25:14-30; 1 Corinthians 6:2-3; 2 Timothy 2:12; Revelation 20: 4, 22:5).

Right to eat from the tree of life (Revelation 2:7, 22:1-2).

See God face to face (1 Corinthians 13:11-12; Revelation 22:3-5).

Sit with Jesus on His throne (Revelation 3:21).

Wear God's name, Jerusalem's name, and Jesus' new name (Revelation 3:12).

Christians are not of this world; we are from the Kingdom of Heaven. Although we are in this world we are not to set our minds on the things everyone does. We are not to set our minds on the things that everyone else in the world sets their minds on. They worry about what they will eat, wear, and where they will sleep. They focus on their careers, driving nice cars, going on vacations, having a big house etc. because this is what the world has persuaded them is all they have to look forward to. The Christians focus is supposed to be on God and all those things that He promised us. Therefore, we live for Him and look forward to those things that are above instead of what is below. Our inheritance is eternal, not temporary. All of the things on earth are temporary.

WHY HOPE IS SO IMPORTANT

Hope is important because it will determine whether or not we will experience true joy and how much of it. What this means is, if you hope in materialistic things, when you do not receive them, you will be upset, disappointed, miserable, and hopeless. On the other hand, if you obtain them, you'll be happy, optimistic, and in high spirits. Still, when they are taken away, you'll be upset, disappointed, miserable, and hopeless again.

To hope in materialistic things or favorable outcomes and circumstances is to have the hope of the world. Contrary to the hope of the world is the hope of the Lord, which is a sure and unfailing thing. It is eternal. The one who hopes in Him and His eternal promises will find eternal joy because this is what it produces. Where the physical things provide us happiness, the eternal (unseen) things of God provide us with eternal joy; a joy no one can ever take away from us.

The hope of the Lord offers a joy that is not dependent upon favorable outcomes and circumstances; it is dependent upon the salvation God has given us and the promises that come with it. Since what has been given to us is of God we can never lose it and no one can take it away from us. Furthermore, since it is eternal, so is the joy it produces. As a result, we can rejoice in the good or bad because our hope brings us a joy that allows us to endure any situation or circumstance without changing. In fact, those things that make life difficult for us will then have its purpose in our lives without hindrance; working in us the patience we need to develop the character God wants and continually confirming the hope in us as that character is manifested daily. [56] This is why hope is so important.

CONCLUSION

Biblical Hope is:
Trustful expectation of receiving what God has promised.

---

[56] Romans 5:1-5

Trustful expectation in what we do not see (eternal things). Based on the word of God.

Q & A on HOPE

1. What is hope? What is the difference between hope and faith?
2. What should we hope for? What shouldn't we hope for?
3. When you are hoping for something, what role does patience play?
4. Why is hope so important to the Christian walk?
5. What example or testimony do you have for when you have hoped for something, and it happened? Were you disappointed?
6. Based on the author's definition of hope, where did you place your hope, when you were disappointed?
7. How is hope spoken about in the New Testament?

_____

_____

_____

Chapter 6

GRACE

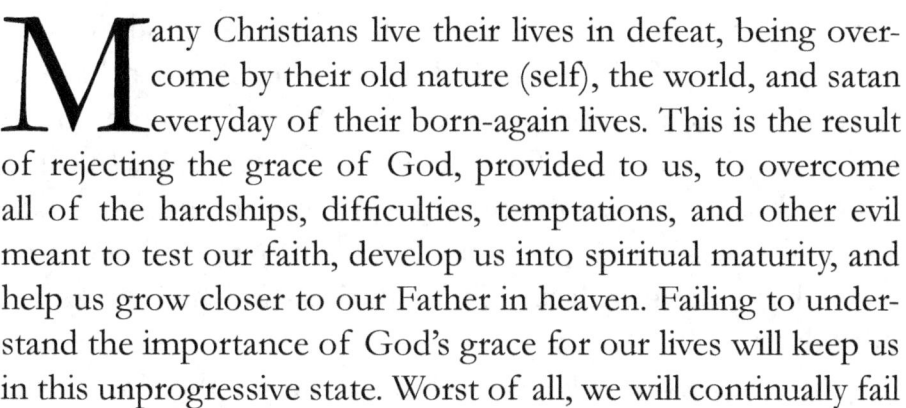

Many Christians live their lives in defeat, being overcome by their old nature (self), the world, and satan everyday of their born-again lives. This is the result of rejecting the grace of God, provided to us, to overcome all of the hardships, difficulties, temptations, and other evil meant to test our faith, develop us into spiritual maturity, and help us grow closer to our Father in heaven. Failing to understand the importance of God's grace for our lives will keep us in this unprogressive state. Worst of all, we will continually fail to succeed in the things of God.

The Christian has satan, self, and the world against them, every day, working hard to keep them from growing in every aspect of their faith. The more we surrender to them, the longer we will experience defeat. Our new nature (new life) is weakened when we continually give in to Satan, Self, and the World. In other words, surrendering to these three will prolong our new nature from growing and keep us from experiencing the abundant life given to us in Christ Jesus.

Defeat, misery, despair, and its other companions is the product of surrendering to satan, self, and the world. This is why the grace of God is so important. His grace will allow all of us to overcome satan, self, and the world. It will allow us to grow closer to Him, grow in spiritual maturity, and serve our purpose in this world. God's grace is the means by which we will find true peace, joy, strength, and success. Therefore, I begin this lesson with an explanation on what is the grace of God.

WHAT IS THE GRACE OF GOD?

God's grace is the fact that we have received and are currently receiving His undeserved favor. The Christian has entered the grace of God when God loved and accepted them by Jesus Christ and His finished works for salvation. In other words, those of us who were found guilty, (sentenced to death and hell because of our sins), God had loved and accepted through our faith in Jesus Christ and His finished works for our salvation.

God gave his only begotten Son to die for the sins of the world so that whoever receives Him and trusts Him as Lord and Savior can be justified, redeemed, forgiven, sanctified, purified, reconciled to Him, saved from death and hell, become born-again, accepted as His children, and blessed with eternal life. This is God's gift to those who have trusted in Christ as Lord and Savior. In other words, God has done for us what we did not deserve and could not earn by any good deeds or behavior. Therefore, it was by His grace that we received it at all.[57] This is the grace of God.

God provides for us according to what we need, even though we do not deserve it and cannot earn it. To understand and experience it, we must first understand how we can receive this grace and have access to it.

BY GRACE YOU WERE SAVED

God's gift of salvation is the key to understanding His grace because it was by grace you were saved and have been given access to such great riches. God saved you from the penalty of your sins (death, hell, darkness, destruction). This means that you've escaped the wrath of God. It means that, in God's eyes, you no longer stand guilty of your sins or sentenced to the penalty that they carry. Be joyful! You no longer owe Him for your sinful ways and lifestyle because the guilt and sentence was accepted and fully paid for by Jesus Christ. That is how you received the grace of God.

This grace vindicated you through Jesus Christ and allowed God to trade in your fallen (sinful) nature for a new (sinless) nature in Jesus Christ. This means that in God's eyes, you're seen as being pure and holy because you are covered by the blood sacrifice of His sinless Son. It means that you are accepted as His child and reunited with Him. In other words, because of your sins, you were an enemy of God and therefore, cut off from His presence and favor. However, because of the grace that you received from Jesus Christ, you have become a

---

[57]   Romans 3:24,5:10,8:15,23; 1 Corinthians 6:11; Ephesians 1:7, 2:8; Colossians 1:14; 1 Peter 1:22; Revelation 5:9

member of His family and can now enjoy access to His grace in your time of need.[58]

By His grace, you have become a child of God. This means that God has separated you from all those who are not His (unbelievers) and all that has nothing to do with Him (worldliness). Furthermore, He has united you with all those who are His (His church) and positioned you over all that is His. This means that you have purpose in this world and responsibility in His Kingdom.

Look at it this way. Your Father in Heaven is the KING of Kings and LORD of Lords. He is holy, true, righteous, just, faithful, merciful, loving, peaceful, joyful, compassionate, long suffering, meek, self-controlled, good, kind, humble, etc. You have become His child; therefore, you represent Him and reflect who He is to the world. This is what He's done for you through His grace and because He did this for you, you now have access to the riches of His grace.

BY GRACE YOU WERE CALLED

It is very important to know and understand that God called us into this salvation by grace. In view of the fact that we have received our salvation by grace and not hard work, it is by grace that we can work out (experience) our salvation.[59]

Many Christians receive their salvation by faith and grace and then think that they now have to work hard to manifest it. In other words, they believe that they have to do lots of reading, going to church, praying, good deeds, etc. in order to

---

[58] Romans 5:1
[59] Ephesians 2:9; 2 Timothy 1:9; Philippians 2:12-13

be a better Christians. While it is true that all of these tools are helpful in our spiritual development, we should not think that this is the way to become a Christian.

You are already a Christian if you've repented of your sinful lifestyle and trusted in Jesus for your salvation. Others simply continue in sin and bondage, unable to experience their salvation. Yet, they believe that God is going to work out their salvation while they continue living sinfully.

We must understand that we are under grace and not under works, the law, or the rule of sin. To understand this is to afford ourselves the opportunity to work out (experience) our own salvation, grow in spiritual maturity, our relationship with God, and our purpose in the Kingdom of God.

We are called to surrender to GOD. This means to surrender our body, soul, and minds as instruments of righteousness instead of sin.[60] This begins with the mind, which affects the soul, and drives the body,[61] but depends on the grace of God, which is ministered to us through the Spirit of grace.[62] This raises the question, what about the fact that we keep struggling with sin even though we do not want to sin anymore?

WHERE SIN ABOUNDS, GRACE ABOUNDS EVEN MORE

What prevents us from growing in spiritual maturity, our relationship with God, our purpose in the Kingdom of God, and experiencing our salvation, is a matter of faith. You must

---

[60] Romans 6:13-19
[61] Romans 12:1-2
[62] Hebrews 10:29

know and <u>act</u> on the fact that no matter how great the sin in your life, God has a greater grace.[63] This means that God's grace is able to help you overcome your struggle with sin, self, the world, and Satan if you *trust, rely,* and *depend* on Him instead of yourself or any other outside source.

You must know and act on the fact that "God is able to make all grace abound toward you: that ye always having all sufficiency in all things, may abound to every good work," (2 Corinthians 9:8). He knows what you are going through. He knows that you may be suffering and what exactly you are in need of. Nevertheless, you must come to Him for help and believe without a doubt that He is a rewarder of those who seek Him.[64]

GRACE THROUGH JESUS CHRIST

Jesus Christ came into the world full of grace and truth.[65] As explained above, it is through Him that we received the grace of God by the gift of salvation. This is important for Christians to understand because, the same grace we relied upon to receive salvation is the same grace we must rely on to experience it. This means that we can do nothing without Him to experience our salvation.[66] However, if we're sticking to Him like glue, He will provide us with all that we need to work out (experience) our salvation and overcome sin, self, the world, and Satan.

---

[63] Romans 5:20-21
[64] James 1:6-8; Hebrews 11:6
[65] John 1:14,17
[66] John 15:5

Furthermore, if we need wisdom, understanding, guidance, or instruction, He has it for us. If we need strength, peace, comfort, or joy, He has it for us. If we're looking for satisfaction, success, and purpose, He has it for us. If we need deliverance, provision, healing, or forgiveness, He has that as well.

What Christians do not realize is that He knows we need all of these things and is ready to provide them for us, but He is waiting on us to go to Him for it. This shows Him just how much we trust, rely, and depend on Him. This is why Peter encouraged us to grow in grace.[67] In other words, He was telling us to grow in the faith of our Lord Jesus the Christ because He gives us grace for grace;[68] meaning that He gives us what we need (grace) for what we obtained from Him through grace (salvation).

When we come to Him in need, we must come to Him in faith as discussed in our previous chapter. We are not to come to Him for the grace we might need for tomorrow, next week, or next year. It must be for the here and now. It must be today and only for today because today is all He gave us and all He provides for.[69] Yet, when we do come to Him, it must be in confidence. We must be confident that He is waiting for us and ready to care for our needs. This is why He gave us access to His throne of grace for our time of need.[70]

---

[67] 2 Peter 3:18
[68] John 1:16
[69] Matthew 6:25-32
[70] Romans 5:2; Hebrews 4:16

GRACE TO THE HUMBLE

All men and women in the world, whether they believe in God and have received Jesus Christ as their Lord and Savior or not, receive grace from God. The believer, however, receives more grace because they have received salvation and now have access to the throne of God through Jesus Christ our Lord. The non-believer does not. The grace they received is limited by the mercy of God, such as food, patience, shelter, clothing, and preservation of life.

This mercy is based on the hope that they will come to repentance and trust in His Son Jesus Christ for salvation. Unfortunately, they have been cut off from having their prayers heard, which means that they have been cut off from more grace because of their prideful and stubborn attitude when it comes to sin and salvation. They must humble themselves enough to repent of their sinful ways and lifestyle and admit that they need Jesus Christ for deliverance from the penalty of their sins and wrath of God.

This act of humility is an acknowledgement that they can't escape the penalty of sin without Him. This is a gift of God, which is His grace. Without this gift there is no access to the rest of His grace because His grace is meant for salvation. Once we have received the gift of salvation, we will then have access to His grace.[71]

The same way un-believers must humble themselves, so must the Christian in order to receive grace. We cannot obtain anything from God without first recognizing that we need Him, can't do anything without Him, and do not deserve any-

---

[71] James 4:6; 1 Peter 5:5

thing good from Him. This is the kind of humility that God looks for from those who need His grace.

Today, too many Christians are mentally and emotionally rich. They act as if they can work out their own salvation by themselves. These are those trying to sin not, obey the law of God, and perform as many good deeds as they can. All the while they neglect God, their relationship with Him, and His Church. Someone described this state of mind as being so mentally rich that they do not realize how spiritually poor they have become. In other words, they are so prideful that they disqualify themselves from God's grace. Others, on the other hand, can't rely on themselves, the Church, or God to work out their own salvation. In fact, they'll admit their spiritual poverty, but cannot humble themselves enough to come to God and accept His help. They refuse the gift of God's grace.

In any sense, the gift of salvation depends upon the grace of God and in order to receive that grace, we must humble ourselves before Him. This act of humility should reflect an attitude of total dependency, reliance, and trust in Jesus Christ, because we acknowledge that we can't do anything without Him. In humility, prayer, and faith, we can approach His throne of grace and mercy in our time of need.

Christ sits at the right hand of the Father, waiting for us to come to Him for the grace we need. Through the Holy Spirit and His Angels, we will receive that grace so that we are able to grow closer to God, grow in spiritual maturity, overcome evil, and serve our intended purpose in this life. Therefore, we must grow in grace.

GROW IN GRACE & KNOWLEDGE OF CHRIST

We have reached the point in this lesson where we must now focus on why it is important for us to grow in grace. To grow in grace means to develop into a mature believer through our dependence on Jesus Christ. In other words, we are to bear much fruit in this new life that was given to us. This life is supposed to produce the fruit of love, joy, peace, patience, kindness, goodness, faithfulness, gentleness, and self-control.[72] In the book of John, Jesus the Christ said, "I am the vine; you are the branches. If a man remains in me and I in him, he will bear much fruit; apart from me you can do nothing."[73] Since Jesus is the grace of God given to us, we cannot grow apart from Him, which means that we need to learn how to rely on Him completely.

Peter encouraged us to grow in grace and knowledge of Christ.[74] When Peter encourages us to grow in the knowledge and grace of Jesus the Christ, he is telling us to work on our relationship with Him because it is important for our spiritual growth. The life He gave us is dependent upon Him for growth, so the closer we draw to Him, the more we get to know Him, the stronger our relationship will get with Him. The more we get to know Him, the more we are able to live out the life we've been given.

Grace comes into play as we go about our lives following our Leader. It is like a child following its father. A child is to

---

[72] Galatians 5:22 (NIV)
[73] John 15:5 (NIV)
[74] 2 Peter 3:18

learn from his father, until he begins to talk, think, and act like his father. Eventually, the child will begin to look like his father because of how well He represents him. A child is able to become like and represent his father because he has come to know who his father is, which enlightens him to his potential. However, it is through his complete trust, reliance, and dependence in his father that he is able to become who he is supposed to be. He relies on the help and assistance of his father because he is confident that he can get all that he needs from his father.

In the same way, the more we grow in knowledge and grace of Christ Jesus, the more we will be able to grow in spiritual maturity and our relationship with God. As we grow in these aspects of our salvation, we are able to become fruitful in our lives for the glory of God. We will also be able to serve God with respect and godly fear; our hearts will be established with grace, which those around us will experience because we will have it to give.[75]

CONCLUSION

Grace is:
God's gift and undeserved favor to man through Jesus Christ
The gift of salvation through repentance and faith in Jesus Christ
The gift of new life by which we've been born again
The fact that we have been justified, redeemed, forgiven, sanctified, purified, reconciled to God, rescued from darkness,

---

[75] Hebrews 12:28,13:9; Ephesians 4:29; Colossians 4:6

destruction, death, and hell and have been adopted as His children

The means by which God is able to do all that we need Him to do through our knowledge and faith in Jesus Christ

The means to grow in spiritual maturity, closer to God, and become fruitful in our service to God

Q & A on GRACE

1. What is grace? Where have you noticed grace in your life?
2. Based on the author's definition of grace, have you ever shown anyone grace? If so, who?
3. Does God show grace to believers or unbelievers?
4. What does it mean to have God's grace as a believer?
5. What is the difference between the law and grace?
6. How does humility and grace work hand in hand together?
7. How does grace give you the ability to workout your own salvation?

_____

_____

_____

Chapter 7

TRUTH

Thus far, we have learned about Hell, Salvation, Repentance, Faith, Hope, and Grace. Now, we've reached the subject of Truth, the foundation of all other subjects. For an individual to obtain or receive the truth, someone must speak it into existence, which means that it must come from someone we can *trust, rely,* and *depend* on to tell us the whole truth and not some manipulated or distorted version of it. That person must be a faithful source of truth.

The question then becomes, who is this faithful source of truth who has spoken it into existence. In other words, where does the truth come from?

WHERE DOES TRUTH COME FROM?

There is none, but God, who has spoken the truth into existence and for that reason is the source of truth. This is only possible because He is the Truth and has always existed.[76] What makes Him the faithful source of truth is the fact that He is the all-knowing God, and cannot lie.[77] Thus, we do not have to worry about being deceived, misled, or misinformed on any matter because it is within His nature to tell us the entire truth and nothing but the truth.

Since He is the Truth, every word that proceeds out of His mouth is true. This is precisely how He has provided it for us. What was spoken out of His mouth was clothed with words so that we can receive what He wants us to know. Therefore, truth comes from God and was given to us through His Word, (the Bible). In fact, the Bible informs us that Jesus Christ is the incarnate Word of God, full of truth, and is the truth.[78] Therefore, we can rely on Jesus Christ as the faithful source of truth.

WHAT IS TRUTH?

Truth is the opposite of lying. A liar is a person who does not speak or hold on to the truth. The Bible informs us that those who lie and do not hold on to the truth are children of the devil because there is no truth in him and he is, "a liar and the father of lies."[79] God is the Truth and the possessor of it. He is not like Satan or man that lies.

However, we can not possess God as a tangible thing. This is why He gave us the truth clothed in words.[80] We rely on the

---

[76] Deuteronomy 32:4; 2 Samuel 2:28; Psalm 91:4; Psalm 119:142, 151, 160; Isaiah 65:16; Jeremiah 10:10; John 17:17
[77] Numbers 23:19
[78] John 1:1; John 1:14; John 14:6
[79] John 8:44
[80] Nehemiah 9:13; Psalm 91:4; Psalm 117:2, 119:30, 160; 2 Timothy 2:13

Bible because this is where the truth has been stored up and preserved for us who desire to know the truth. This does not mean that there is no truth outside of the Bible. It means that there is no truth apart from God, so if there is truth outside of the Bible, its original source could be tied to God.

There are many books, philosophical beliefs, doctrines, etc. that have travelled the world and contain some truth in it. The problem is that man had taken the truth of God and distorted or corrupted it, making it appear as their own or that someone else is the original source and, therefore, use it to lead many astray. There is also the truth that arises from experience, history, and honesty. Specifically, what we are talking about is any truth that agrees and does not stand in contradiction with what the Bible teaches or what God stands for.

Nevertheless, the truth is unpolluted and eternal no matter where it is or who it comes from. It will never change or pass away. This is what we can confidently claim about the Bible. It is the only source of truth that has been confirmed to be trustworthy and dependable upon its application.

HOW CAN WE KNOW THE BIBLE IS TRUE?

The truth is revealed to us when we put it to the test.[81] God has informed us that He is the truth and Jesus Christ is the embodiment of that truth. Through the Bible we have the spoken word of God and Christ, which is why the Bible claims to be the truth. Furthermore, Christ, His apostle John, and Paul said that they have told us the truth.[82]

---
[81] Malachi 3:10; 1 John 4:1
[82] Luke 4:24, 9:27; John 16:7, 19:35; Romans 9:1-2; 2 Corinthians 7:14; 2 Tim-

If someone tells us that they hold the truth, they are telling us the truth, they are not lying, and encourage us to test what has been told to us so that we can prove that they mean what they say, they obviously wish to authenticate themselves. However, to find out, we must test and confirm it for ourselves. This is where faith comes into play. If you are not willing to test it (act on it) then you will never know if it is true or not. To take the Bible seriously and act like we believe it is telling us the truth, is Faith. This is how we can know that the Bible is the truth.

WHY IS THE TRUTH IMPORTANT?

Jesus the Christ is the light of the world and whoever follows after Him will not walk in darkness but have the light of life.[83] Symbolically, truth is the light of life that Jesus refers to. To be without it is to walk in sin, ignorance, blindness, and darkness. This is catastrophic because it could lead to death, destruction, and hell. It was the truth that led us to Jesus Christ and the gift of salvation.[84]

Therefore, the *first* reason truth is important is because it allows us to see things clearly, without a distorted perception. It allows us to discern good and evil, truth and lies, right and wrong, and what is healthy and unhealthy for us. In other words, the truth gives us a sense of reality that is supported by evidence. We see things for what they are and not simply what they appear to be.

---

othy 2:7; Acts 26:25
[83] John 8:12
[84] Romans 10:17

Secondly, for the Christian, the truth is our foundation for life. It is the most trustworthy, reliable and dependable thing that we have to build our lives with. In other words, the truth produces wisdom in our lives, and this is what we use to build our lives.[85] Therefore, truth is important because it will determine the kind of life that a Christian will enjoy.

Lastly, the truth is important for the Christian because it is tied to the promises, blessing, freedom, satisfaction, success, and purpose of the Lord for us.[86] Without it, we cannot lay claim to the things God has for us.

CONCLUSION

Truth is:
God
Jesus Christ
The Holy Spirit
Light of men
The Word of God
The Bible

---

[85] Luke 6:46-49; 1 Corinthians 3:10-12
[86] Matthew 5:6; John 8:32, 14:12-15, 15:1-8; Ephesians 1:3; 2 Peter 1:3-4

Q & A on TRUTH

1. What does the Bible say that truth is?
2. How important is it for the Bible to be true?
3. What is the source of truth?
4. What tests are used to verify truth concerning the Bible?
5. Can truth change?
6. Why is truth so important?
7. Can you live your life without truth?

_____

_____

_____

Chapter 8

PRAYER

In the life of a Christian, prayer is of ultimate importance because of all our needs and the needs of those that we encounter. As explained in our lesson on Salvation, the Christian has been saved from the penalty of sins and given the gift of eternity in heaven. However, while they remain on earth, it is God's will that the Christian grows in knowledge of Him,[87] relation to Him,[88] spiritual maturity,[89] and likeness of Christ.[90] Furthermore, the Christian is expected to learn how-to walk-in faith, grow in the grace of God, fulfill God's commandments, and be fruitful in their ministry. For these reasons, we must learn the importance of prayer and grow in our prayer life.

---

[87] 2 Peter 3:18
[88] James 4:8
[89] Hebrews 5:11-14, 6:1; Colossians 1:9-11
[90] Romans 8:29

Prayer is a major part of the Christian life. It is an essential element for developing our identity and growing closer to God. We (Christians) are children of God,[91] the light of the world, and salt of the earth.[92] We are representatives of our Lord in humility, mercy, peace, joy, faith, love, truth, patience, self-control, contentment, meekness, kindness, gentleness, holiness, righteousness, and pureness of heart.[93]

Our Father in heaven knows what we are in need of and that we rely on His assistance to help us live as a child of God. He also desires that we grow in knowledge of Him, relation to Him, spiritual maturity, Christ likeness, and God given purpose. However, we must learn to rely on the grace He has for us. If we do not, we will not receive the help that we need. Thus, it is through *prayer* and *faith* that we are able to activate that grace and receive His assistance. With that said, I begin this lesson with an explanation of what prayer is.

WHAT IS PRAYER?

Prayer is the act by which the Christian humbles themselves before God and expresses their desperate need for Him. In other words, it is an admission of our spiritual poverty. In humility, prayer becomes the line of communication the Christian is given to offer our Father in heaven thanks, praise, confession, intercession, and petitions. It is the way Christians communicate with God (Father, Son, and Holy Spirit) and make known

---

[91] John 1:12-13
[92] Matthew 5:13-16
[93] Matthew 5:3-9; Galatians 5:22-23

our hardships, difficulties, sufferings, needs, and desires. It is the way we receive mercy and grace in our time of need.

WHY IS PRAYER SO IMPORTANT?

Dr. Tony Evans said, "If the new nature that God placed in us at salvation is like an expensive refrigerator that has all the necessary parts to function properly and the Holy Spirit is the power source that makes this new appliance work the way it was designed to work, then prayer is like the wires and connectors through which this power flows and reaches the component parts of our new nature."

The Christian has been born again, of God, and has the seed of God within them. Prayer, then, is important because it is the means by which we remain connected to the source of life inside of us, God. To communicate with Him, is to allow Him to maintain the life He has on earth. Everything on earth was created by God, therefore, can only be sustained by Him. To maintain communication with Him is to allow Him to nurture and care for our life as we remain on this earth.

TO WHOM SHOULD WE PRAY?

Primarily, we should know that we are praying to God (Father, Son, and Holy Spirit). Although they are all equal in nature and one in essence, they have different offices. Thus, depending on what your need is, and who (Father, Son, and Holy Spirit) is in charge of providing for that need, this will determine who it is that you should be praying to. This is why it is important for every Christian to get to know the Father, Son, and Holy Spirit personally and intimately.

Nevertheless, Jesus has instructed us to pray to our Father in heaven. Therefore, we should not trouble ourselves on the question, "Who should we pray to." If you are not certain, just address our Father in Jesus' name until you get to know all of them.

HOW DO WE PRAY?

It is of the utmost importance for all Christians to understand that the way to pray is in the Holy Spirit,[94] through Jesus the Christ,[95] and most importantly, in the name of Jesus our Lord and Savior.[96] What does this all mean?

First of all, what it means to pray in the Holy Spirit, is to make sure (through self-examination of our heart and mind) that we are not in the wrong spirit when we pray. Many times, we communicate things to God that are not coming from a good place inside of us. We can ask Him for things that come from a place of selfishness, greed, lust, pride, anger, etc. This is what we want to make sure we are not doing. The best way to make sure that we are in the right Spirit is to examine ourselves and ask why we feel how we feel, why we want what we want, and in that conclusion, check what His word has to say about the matter we are bringing to Him in prayer.

Secondly to pray through Jesus Christ means that we are aware that we cannot approach the throne of our Father in

---

[94] Ephesians 6:18
[95] Romans 1:8; Colossians 3:17
[96] John 14:13-14

Heaven in our own right, but only through the permission and righteousness of Jesus Christ who gave His life for us and is seated as our Mediator at the right hand of the Father.

<u>Lastly</u>, when we do anything in someone's name, it means that we are doing it with their permission, under their authority, and as their representatives. The three always go hand in hand. They are not apart from each other.

This last one seems to be one of the most difficult things for Christians to understand. To do anything in the name of another person requires that you have their authority and permission to do so. It requires that you do what you have been called to do as they would. This is what it means to pray to God in the name of Jesus. Once you can effectively represent your Lord and Savior, you can effectively pray in His name. In prayer, your words and heart's desire ought to reflect the mind and heart of Christ more and more each day you get to know Him.

Think of it in this way; say you are hired to be the manager of a highly successful business company. Although you have no clue as to how this business operates successfully, this is not a problem because you have the owner of the business, who started this thing from the ground up and made it successful, willing to teach you everything that you need to know to run his company successfully.

To assure your success, the owner of the company gives you complete access to all of the knowledge and understanding that you need to familiarize yourself with his business. He offers you the opportunity to follow his lead (to learn from Him and the way he runs His business) until you are able to run the company on your own. He assures you that if you are careful to do as he does, you'll be a worthy representative of his.

This is how you become a representative of Christ and can effectively pray in His name. Once you learn how to run his business the way He runs it, you can fulfill your responsibilities as the "manager" of His business. However, this will take time, effort, and diligence, so do not give up or be discouraged if it takes longer than you expect. With this knowledge and understanding on prayer, let us explore the application of prayer, or should I say, "how to pray."

When the disciples asked Jesus to teach them how to pray, Jesus taught them, first, to pray in secret and not to use repetitive words. The secrecy Jesus is talking about is dealing with the desire in man's heart to be seen by God as opposed to man when we pray. In other words, prayer is about God hearing you, seeing you, and speaking to you; it is not about anyone around you. Thus, we ought to keep it between God and us. Do not do it for human recognition.

Jesus also instructed us to not use vain repetitions. This is because prayer is not only about intimacy with God, but also about being real with Him. Come to Him in complete transparency. You should be coming to Him because there is a real problem, need, and desire. Do not come to Him speaking all kinds of nonsense. We do not have to sound good, speak many words, or repeat some traditional prayer. Just say what you need or what the problem is. Remember, He already knows. Jesus said, "Your Father knows the things you have need of before you ask Him," (Matthew 6:8).

"<u>Our Father</u> in <u>heaven hallow be thy name</u>, let <u>your kingdom come and will be done</u> on earth as it is in heaven. <u>Give us this day our daily bread and forgive us our debts</u> as we forgive our debtors. <u>Lead us not into temptation</u> but <u>deliver us from evil</u>," (Matthew 6:9-13).

This is the example He set for us, but it is only a template for prayer. You are to ask yourself, "What do these words mean to me? What is my heart communicating to my Father in heaven when I utter these words to Him?" They are not to be empty words, but meaningful. Here is an example of what I am referring to:

<u>Our Father in heaven</u>: When we communicate with our Father, it is important to understand who He is to you and who you are to Him. He is not just God to us. He is not unknown or unfamiliar. He is our Father, and you are His child. We ought to approach Him with this attitude. In other words, do not act as if you are speaking to a stranger. Also, recognize that He is not an earthly Father. He is your heavenly Father. Do not compare Him to an imperfect man. He is the greatest Father anyone can have. Think about that.

<u>Hallow be thy name</u>: Honor His name for the holiness and greatness that it is. Think of who He is, (good, kind, meek, pure, merciful, gracious, patient, faithful, loving, true, unchanging, unfailing, all powerful, all knowing, all present, etc.) In all of this, He is unlike anyone that we know. Why? Because in all of His ways, He is holy, perfect, and just. Get familiar with His character and attributes. Reflect on all He has done, all He's doing, and all He will do. Praise/thank Him for that. Acknowledge that there is none like Him.

<u>Your Kingdom come, your will be done, on earth as in heaven</u>: Man's rule on earth has been the cause of much suffering. There has been too much injustice, inequality, discrimination, violence, war, and oppression under the authority of man. Therefore, our Father's rule and authority is needed on earth, in the lives of every man, women, and child. Without it, evil will triumph. We want His will to be done on earth and in

our lives because only He can assure the best for us. We long for the day when all the evil, pain, sickness, suffering, misery, and death that we experience is no more. Therefore, we ask that our Father's rule and authority come, and His will be done here on earth as it is in heaven. This of course depends on members of His church to be obedient and faithful to Him so that He can make this happen through us as well.

<u>Give us this day our daily bread:</u> The Christian is not to worry or live for food, shelter, or clothing. In other words, we are not to live worrying about taking care of ourselves. We are to trust that our Father cares enough about us to take care of our needs everyday He gives us on earth. Instead of focusing on ourselves, we are to focus on the purpose for our lives on earth, the day our Father has given us to serve that purpose and trust the He will sustain us as we pursue that purpose. Each day has its own hardships, difficulties, and challenges. When they confront us in our daily living, we are able to handle them according to the word of God. Thus, when we ask for our daily bread, it is not just to sustain us physically, but also spiritually, which is just as important if not more important. Jesus the Christ has said that man does not live by bread alone (physical sustenance), but by every word proceeding out of the mouth of God. However, if you are hungry then ask, seek, and knock…He will provide.

<u>Forgive us our debts as we forgive our debtors:</u> On a daily basis, the Christian sins against our Father in a moral and spiritual manner. The important thing here is to remain in fellowship with our Father in heaven because sin places us at a distance from Him. He is a Holy Father, who cannot abide in or around sin. Thus, the blood of Jesus cleanses us daily and keeps us in perfect harmony with our Father. Furthermore, as

our Father accepts us with our imperfections, errors, and faults, we must ask ourselves if we are doing the same for those who reveal their imperfections, errors, and faults to us. We must ask ourselves if we are loving others as He loves us and being merciful as He is merciful to us, because it is what He expects of His children and representatives. In other words, we are expected to give others what we are asking or expecting of Him. Thus, individual forgiveness also depends on our willingness to forgive others. Our Father expects this from us.

<u>Lead us not into temptation:</u> This does not mean that our Father entices us with evil that triggers our weaknesses and leads us to sin. Although He will allow our ability to endure and overcome temptation to be tested, He will not tempt us with evil Himself. This evil will only come from within us or the evil around us. Nevertheless, He controls and rules over every little detail, situation, or circumstance in the Christian life. Christ recognized this important factor when He prayed that "the cup" He had to drink be removed from Him.[97] However, it was needed, so He had to endure the pain, anguish and death that filled that cup. What we are asking Him is that we are not tempted beyond what our faith can handle and that we are not overcome by it.

<u>Deliver us from evil:</u> Satan is devising schemes and plans to steal our love, kill our joy, and destroy our peace. He wants to entice and lure us into sinning, bind us by sin, and defeat us by sin. His attacks are spiritual, although his tools may be physical. He targets our mind and heart to destroy the soul. We need our Father to protect and deliver us from his evil schemes and attacks.

---

[97] Matthew 26:39

WHAT ARE THE FUNDAMENTALS OF PRAYER?

There are four elements of prayer that should be uttered from the believer's mouth and heart to our Father. The prayer we just explored has all of these elements incorporated into it. These elements are: **1.)** Thanksgiving/Praise[98]; **2.)** Confession[99]; **3.)** Intercessions[100]; and **4.)** Petitions[101]

WHAT ARE OUR HUMAN FUNDAMENTALS FOR PRAYER?

Every believer must examine him or herself to make sure they are in the *spirit* before entering prayer. In other words, be sure that we are not lacking any of the following:

Fear of the Lord (Psalm 145:19; Prover 1:29).
Faith (Mark 11:24; James 1:6, 5:15).
Humility (2 Chronicles 7:14, 33:12).
Repentance (2 Chronicles 6:37; Acts 3:19).
Undivided heart (Deuteronomy 4:29; Jeremiah 29:13).
Sinlessness (Psalm 66:18-19; Isaiah 1:15-16; John 9:31).
Selflessness (Luke 18:9-14; James 4:3).
Doubtlessness (Matthew 21:21; James 1:5-6).
Forgiveness (Matthew 6:14-15).
Confidence (Ephesians 3:12; Hebrews 10:19-35, 1 John 3:21).
Persistence (Luke 11:5-10, 18:1-7; 1 Thessalonians 5:17).

---

[98] Psalm 136; Matthew 6:9; Philippians 4:6
[99] Psalm 51; Matthew 6:12; 1 John 1:9
[100] Psalm 122:6-9; Matthew 6:10
[101] Psalm 27:7-12; Matthew 6:10,26:39-42

Sincerity (Matthew 6:5-8).
God's will (Matthew 26:42; 1 John 5:14).
Obedience (1 John 3:22).

If we are not in this spirit when we pray, then we ought to consider asking our father to assist us in developing this spirit. We may have to seek assistance in developing this kind of spirit for a long time. However, we must remember that we have already obtained this Spirit in Christ. These spiritual qualities reflect who you are as a born-again child of God. Therefore, you are able to express these qualities if you are willing to make the necessary sacrifices and efforts required of you to develop the new nature in you.

CONCLUSION

Prayer is the way Christians communicate with God (Father, Son, and Holy Spirit).

It is the way we make known our hardships, difficulties, sufferings, needs, and desires to God so that we may receive the mercy and grace needed for our circumstances or situations.

It is the line of communication the Christian has been given to offer up thanksgiving, confession, intercession, and petitions to God.

It is the form in which the Christian humbles themselves before God and confesses their desperate need of Him.

Q & A on PRAYER

1. What does it mean to pray?
2. What is the purpose of prayer?
3. Why is prayer so important in the believer's life?
4. To whom should you pray to?
5. How does Romans 1:8, Colossians 3:17 and John 14:13-14 tell us we should pray? What does this mean to you according to the scripture?
6. In Mattew 6:5-8, what are we taught about praying? (Explain in your own words).
7. In Matthew 6:9-15, is Jesus telling us to pray exactly like this? If so, explain why. If not, explain why?
8. What are the 4 fundamentals of prayer?
9. Name 7 human fundamentals for prayer.
10. What is the main thing that resonated with you in this subject?

_____

_____

_____

Chapter 9

FORGIVENESS

It is especially important that Christians keep in their hearts and in their minds that God has forgiven us because Jesus Christ bore our sins and died for us. He lifted up the penalty, punishment, and legal obligation we have incurred because of our sinful ways and has taken it all away from us.

Given that He accomplished this for us we have been freed of sin and the wrath of God, redeemed of our fallen nature, accepted by God as His children, and blessed beyond what we deserve. Furthermore, we are able to access the riches of His grace, which allows us to receive of Him all that we need, including more forgiveness for our future errors, weaknesses, and faults. That's right! We have been given room for error and weaknesses in our new relationship with God (our Father) without having to fear suffering any consequences, thanks to what Jesus Christ has done for us.

We must bear this in mind and heart because in this world, we will encounter people who will hurt us, offend us, disgrace us, and cause us to suffer. They may be family, friends, enemies, or strangers. It may be intentional or unintentional. Regardless of whom it comes from, how it comes, or how it affects us, we must know how to respond to it and why we should respond in such a manner. Forgiveness is the response.

FORGIVENESS

Biblically, the meaning of forgiveness is "to lift" (a burden, weight, or penalty), "to bear" or "to take away." In the Old Testament, we read about the necessity for a sacrificial lamb and/or scapegoat for the forgiveness of sins. That lamb or scapegoat "bore" the sins of God's people, according to His requirement.[102] In the New Testament God's forgiveness is expressed by the fact that Jesus Christ bore our sins and took them away in fulfillment of God's plan to restore a fallen humanity.[103]

In the Merriam Webster Dictionary, forgiveness is defined in the following manner: 1.) To give up resentment of; 2.) Pardon/ Absolve; 3.) to grant relief from payment of something; 4.) the will or ability to forgive; and 5.) allowing room for error or weakness. These are the definitions of forgiveness that we will visit in this lesson since they are all based on the Biblical definition of forgiveness and give us a better understanding on how it relates to us. These descriptions of forgiveness allow us to learn how to forgive others as our heavenly Father has forgiven us.

---

[102] Leviticus 16:22
[103] Holman Illustrated Bible Dictionary, 1 Peter 2:24; 1 John 3:5; Luke 22:34-71; Isaiah 53:12

HOW DO WE FORGIVE?

1. <u>To give up resentment</u>: The first expression of forgiveness we receive from the dictionary is the decision to give up resentment. Resentment is an expression of indignation towards someone, which describes the anger one feels towards another that arises when something unjust, hurtful, disgraceful, or wrong occurred. This is a natural response, since no one desires that someone causes them to experience these things. In fact, we can say that indignation is our godly response to evil since God hates evil.

Therefore, you should hate the evil done to you.[104] However, this does not mean you should allow it to go untreated inside of you and allow it to control you. Ephesians 4:31-32 tells us, "Let all bitterness, and wrath, and anger, and clamor, and evil speaking, be put away from you, with all malice; and be ye kind one to another, tenderhearted, *forgiving* one another, even as God for Christ's sake hath forgiven you."

Furthermore, the Hebrew writer encourages that we, "Follow peace with all men, and holiness, without which no man shall see the Lord; looking diligently lest any man fail of the grace of God; lest any root of bitterness springing up trouble you, and thereby many be defiled," (Hebrews 12:14-15). Therefore, we are told that if we do not treat it, it can become trouble for us. The signs are bitterness, wrath, anger, evil speaking, and malice to name a few. These are signs of a developing problem occurring in you.

Putting it away from you through kindness and forgiveness is the way to treat the issue before it becomes a problem. We

---

[104] Psalm 97:10; Amos 5:15; Romans 12:9

are called to overcome evil and not to allow it to overcome us, which is what would happen if we chose not to give up resentment. If we decide when someone hurts, disrespects, or disappoints us, to make ourselves feel better through vengeance, alcohol, or drugs, evil will overcome us.

Those responses reveal that we have allowed some kind of bitterness, wrath, anger, clamor, evil, or malice to pollute our minds and hearts to the point that it produces corrupt fruit out of us. In this process, we give up the love, joy, peace, and the other fruit of the Spirit given to us by Christ our Lord.[105]

In Matthew 5:5-9, we are informed on who the blessed ones of the Lord are. The blessed of the Lord is meek (who possess strength to endure suffering without resentment), the hungry and the thirsty for righteousness, the merciful, the pure in heart (those being conformed to the image of Christ), and the peacemaker (who desire to be at peace with God and all men). What this means is that we can choose to live victoriously by giving up resentment.

2. <u>Pardon or Absolve:</u> The second expression of forgiveness given to us is the decision to free someone from a penalty, punishment, consequence, or legal obligation they have incurred for their wrongful, unjust, offensive, or disgraceful act. Though they may not deserve it, this act of forgiveness is a complete act of love, mercy, and grace.

This act of forgiveness has nothing to do with what we think, feel, or desire. Instead, it has to do with what we have received from God through Jesus Christ. As explained above, Jesus Christ "bore" our sins, its penalty, punishment, consequence, and legal obligation from us and "took it all away"

---

[105] Galatians 5:22-23

from us. Since we have received such a loving, merciful, and gracious gift, we pass it forward to others who need it as we needed it.

3. <u>To Grant Relief from Payment of Something:</u> To grant someone relief from a payment they owe you for what they have done is another act of love, mercy, and grace. Like the decision to pardon someone and absolve them, this too has to do with the relief Jesus Christ gave us from the debt we owed God. Due to the sins that we have committed against ourselves, others, and God, we owed Him our very souls. That was the price of our debt.[106] Thankfully, however, Jesus Christ relieved us of that debt.

This relief is acquired through the fruit of repentance. Just as we turned to Christ in regret and remorse seeking relief from the payment that we could not afford to pay off, so is this relief acquired by anyone who desires it. Where there is regret and remorse there must be relief. It does not matter who is the one seeking relief or how big of a debt they owe. The only thing that matters is the fact that we are able to relieve them of the debt they cannot pay off.[107]

4. <u>The Will or Ability to Forgive:</u> The will or ability to forgive someone has been given to us by the grace bestowed upon us through Jesus Christ the Lord. This ability must be exercised responsibly and should not be used to lord over someone and keep them bound, captive, imprisoned, or enslaved to us. When we were forgiven by God, He delivered us from sin

---

[106] Romans 6:23
[107] Matthew 18:27

so that we may be free, born again, redeemed, and raised up in newness of life.[108]

Being children of God, the ability or will to forgive has been placed in us to bring pleasure, honor, and glory to Him along with every other good fruit.[109] The act of forgiveness allows us to express and demonstrate the love, mercy, and grace of God to the world.[110] Therefore, although it may hurt to be wronged, offended, and made to suffer injustice, we have the ability to suffer-long, be merciful, and forgive like our God. When we exercise this ability responsibly, we please, honor, and glorify our God.

5. <u>Allowing Room for Error or Weakness:</u> Finally, brethren, let us deeply consider this expression of forgiveness because it is one that depicts the type of relationship we have entered with God and the reason that we are able to build or enjoy such a good relationship with Him. This expression of forgiveness has allowed us to obtain forgiveness for our errors and weaknesses, daily, without the worry of our Father in heaven changing towards us and ending our relationship with Him.[111]

In any relationship we enter, we must bear in mind that not only are we imperfect, but so are the people we encounter or share a relationship with. It is precisely for this reason that we must allow room (grace) in our relationships and associations with others for errors and weaknesses. We all make mistakes, have faults, weaknesses, and flaws that have caused our God to suffer and sacrifice for us. Yet, He does not hold that against us out of love, mercy, compassion, and grace.

---

[108] John 1:12-13,3:3-5; 2 Corinthians 5:17-18
[109] Galatians 5:22-23
[110] Numbers 14:18
[111] 1 John 1:9

Therefore, we too should be ready and willing to suffer for others imperfection. They may cause us emotional, mental, or even physical suffering. We may have to sacrifice what we think, feel, or desire for their sake. Nevertheless, this is the cost of love, a love that is manifested through forgiveness. Jesus has commanded us to love one another as He has.[112] In Him, there is no condemnation.[113] Freely ye have received, freely give.[114]

God expects us to accept people as they are (imperfect with errors and weaknesses) and be willing to love them despite their short comings. He also expects us to remember that He accepts and loves us despite our short comings. We can always count on Him to never change towards us because of our imperfection. He has accepted us as we are and is ready to forgive when we fall short. [115]

As children of God, when the errors or weakness in others we associate with, share a relationship with, or encounter appear we must remember that we are the same. We also must remember our relationship with God. This means that we are allowing room in our relationships for errors and weaknesses without allowing them to be a reason for us to change the nature of our relationship. If we do, forgiving them will be easier.

WHY IS FORGIVENESS IMPORTANT?

Today, many Christians are living in a spiritual prison due to the unforgiveness harbored in their hearts. They live miserable, contentious, combative, bitter, angry lives and are full of

---

[112] John 15:12
[113] Romans 8:1
[114] Matthew 10:8
[115] 1 Corinthians 13:4-8

resentment. They are tortured by these thoughts and feelings that are brought upon them by unforgiveness because they refuse to free themselves of it all by simply forgiving the person(s) that hurt them, wronged them, or caused them to suffer.

In addition to this, an unforgiving person can cause others to experience their misery, contention, aggression, bitterness, anger, and resentment. They can cause pain, injury, and other afflictions upon others due to unforgiveness.

An unforgiving mind, heart, and attitude will keep us bound by the evil it comes from. Unforgiveness is intolerance, merciless, pitiless, remorseless, vindictiveness, ruthlessness, callousness, or indifference. These are contrary to love. To develop such a mind, heart and attitude is to be caged, enslaved, and held captive by the evil it produces. This means that we will be controlled by this evil. Our choices and decisions will be influenced or encouraged by it. This could be very destructive.

Therefore, the *first* reason forgiveness is important is because it allows us to be free of evil and its destructive fruit so that we are able to be constructive with our lives and the lives of others.

Secondly, unforgiveness can not only lead to destruction, but also bears the fruit of resentment, bitterness, misery, indignation, and wrath, which can bring self-destruction. Forgiveness relieves us from experiencing such evil. No one wants to hold on to anything that is self-defeating.

Therefore, the *second* reason forgiveness is important is because it allows us to enjoy the love, joy, peace, mercy, and grace God has for us without having to worry about it being taken away by misery, contention, confrontation, bitterness, anger, and resentment.

Jesus Christ has called us to be His representative, to grow in relation to Him, grow in spiritual maturity, fulfill our purpose, and bear much fruit for His glory. If we are not following His examples, such as forgiving, we are hindering ourselves from fulfilling our calling.

If we are being disobedient to Him, this is sin, which means that our fellowship will be broken. However, we learn in 1 John 1:9 that He is faithful and just to forgive us our sins if we ask for it. Our Lord has made it plain to us, when He taught us how to pray, that we should ask our heavenly Father, "Forgive us our debts as we forgive our debtors." He made it very clear that if we do not forgive others, our heavenly Father will not forgive us.[116] This means that we will be broken in fellowship with Him because we have chosen not to forgive.

Lastly, the reason forgiveness is so important is threefold: 1) We cannot receive forgiveness from God unless we forgive; 2) We need forgiveness from God in order to be in unbroken fellowship with Him and receive of His mercy and grace in our time of need; and 3) Without the mercy and grace of God, we cannot be His representatives, grow in relation to Him, grow in spiritual maturity, fulfill our purpose, and bear much fruit for His glory.

<u>CONCLUSION</u>

Forgiveness means:
To lift (as a burden or weight)
To bear (upon yourself)
To take away (like a debt or penalty)

---

[116] Matthew 6:12-15

To give up resentment
Pardon/Absolve
To grant relief from payment of something
Allowing room for error or weakness

Q & A on **FORGIVENESS**

1. What does forgiveness mean?
2. How does one forgive?
3. What description of forgiveness can you relate to? (Explain in your own words).
4. Why is forgiveness important? (Explain in your own words).
5. What did Jesus say about forgiving in Matthew 6:12-15? (Explain in your own words why this is important or if you feel it is not).
6. What does forgiveness mean to you? (Explain).

_____

_____

_____

Chapter 10

LOVE

Within this book, you have learned about Hell, Salvation, Repentance, Faith, Hope, Grace, Truth, Prayer, and Forgiveness. These subjects are vital to know and apply in our Christian lives if we desire to represent our Lord, grow in our relationship with Him, grow in spiritual maturity, fulfill our purpose, and bear much fruit for His glory. This next subject is the final one of this book, because after obtaining a clear understanding of the other subjects and learning how they are to be applied in our lives we are left with the question, what next? The answer is love.

The love you will be learning about in this lesson is not just any kind of love. It is not that weak kind of love that so many people express and experience. The love in this lesson is a love from God. This love is the one that has saved us from Hell, blessed us with Salvation, motivated our repentance, developed our faith, gave us hope, granted us access to grace, freed us from the bondage to sin, delivered us from the path of darkness, gave us an open line of prayer and the opportunity to be forgiven.

This love is the reason we have become children of God, were made at peace with Him, were redeemed, are justified in the sight of God, purified, sanctified, and made righteous. It was the love of God that started the transformative work of salvation in our lives, and it will be the love of God that will see it through until completion. For this reason I have left this subject for last.

Common in the Church of God today is the lack of godly love. Many say that they love as God does and claim they are expressing this love to others, but what others experience is a different kind of love. Most of the time it is a selfish or counterfeit love that is expressed not God's love. This may be acceptable for those outside of God's family, but not for those who are His children and under His divine Lordship. I am referring to Christians.

Knowing and expressing the love of God is essential in the Christian life, yet few understand how important it truly is. The disciple John understood the importance of God's love in the believer's life. In fact, he understood it to be the ultimate proof that a believer in Christ was a child of God. He said that it was proof that we even know God.[117]

In this lesson of love, you will learn 1) What is selfish love; 2) What is counterfeit love; 3) What is true love; 4) Where true love comes from; 5) How can we experience true love; and 6) How to express true love. This is important, not only because of our Christian goals, but because it is proof that we know and belong to God.

---

[117] 1 John 2:10-11; 4:7-13

WHAT IS SELFISH LOVE?

The most popular kind of love expressed and existing in the world today is a selfish love. Selfish love is self-centered. It is all about self with little to no regard for others. In relationships, the person expressing this form of love usually expresses themselves with lots of statements like, "I want," or "I think," or "I feel," or "I do or don't like." This person is mainly motivated by his or her self interest and/or five senses.

The person expressing this type of love often confuses it with preference. In other words, they attribute the same meaning to love as they would their favorite television show, food, snack, and other pleasures in their lives. This means that if the person they claim to love no longer pleases them, as their favorite ice cream would, then the "love" no longer exists.

A person who only knows how to love selfishly will almost always choose to please themselves and not others. This is because selfish love is about receiving, not giving. Even when they choose to put someone else's needs and desires before self, the majority of the time it is not without a selfish motive or interest. Thus, selfish love thinks of its own affairs, troubles, good and pleasure and rarely of the affairs, troubles, good, or pleasures of others. It is willing to sacrifice and suffer for self before others.

WHAT IS COUNTERFEIT LOVE?

Counterfeit love is deceiving because it sometimes looks, feels, and sounds like real love. It shares similar characteristics as true love, but it is not. This is that "I do for you if you do for me," kind of love. Expectations, requirements, stipulations, and preferences is the foundation of this love, so although it may show kindness, generosity, compassion, mercy, encouragement, and other good qualities, once this foundation is tested by hardship, difficulties, trials, and tribulations, the love vanishes, proving that it was never real to begin with.

This type of love is exposed in relationships that test its ability to endure the errors and weaknesses of others. It is quick to withdraw itself and change up when it is convenient for the one dishing it out. In other words, you will only be loved if you do not fail, upset, disappoint, or displease the other, which means that you were never truly loved by them in the first place.

TRUE LOVE

In 1 Corinthians 13:4-8[118] the word of God describes love in the following manner:

Love is patient (willing to suffer a long time for someone.)

Love is kindness (compassionate, thoughtful, sympathetic, considerate, gentle.)

It does not envy (spiteful, greedy, jealous.)

It does not boast (brag, show off, sing your own praises, blow your own horn.)

It is not proud (arrogant, overconfident, bigheaded, swollen with pride, self-righteous, self-important, conceited.)

It is not rude (vulgar, offensive, bad-mannered, discourteous, impolite.)

It is not self-seeking (egotistical, self-absorbed, self-regarding, self-centered, selfish.)

---

[118] 1 Corinthians 13:4-8

It is not easily angered (frustrated, irritated, enraged, annoyed, infuriated.)

It keeps no record of wrong (errors or mistakes.)

Love does not delight in evil but rejoices with truth (It does not take pleasure in wrongdoing but in doing what is right.)

It always protects, always trusts, always hopes, always perseveres.

It never fails.

In other words, the description here is that true love is completely selfless and always willing to sacrifice and suffer. This means that the one offering it must be willing to make the decision to "lay down their life" for the one in need of their love, not because they have asked you to or because they earned it, but because you recognize their need for it. This type of love offers itself for the greater good of others. It places the needs of others before its own. Therefore, in order to meet those needs, it is ready and willing to practice all of the above mentioned.

WHERE DOES TRUE LOVE COME FROM?

God is love. This means that love comes from God. Since He is from everlasting to everlasting (always existing in existence) so is His love. Thus, he is the source of love. God's very essence/nature is love. Anyone who is apart from Him has no access to this love, therefore, is incapable of giving it or sharing it with others. Apart from the source one will be loveless. Anyone seeking to experience this love and offer it must first turn to God and receive His gift of love (Jesus Christ).

HOW TO EXPERIENCE IT

"For God so loved the world, that he gave his only begotten son, that whosoever believeth in him should not perish, but have everlasting life," (John 3:16). God has not only expressed His love for the world, but also given it as a gift for all who wish to experience it through the sacrificial death of His son Jesus Christ.

To experience it, you must receive it. However, to receive it, you must first soften your heart to the gospel (good news) of Jesus Christ's death, burial, and resurrection for our sins and salvation.[119] The scriptures tell us, "Today, if ye will hear his voice, harden not your hearts..." (Hebrews 3:15). A softened heart is what is needed to hear the truth and be enlightened by it. In other words, God's gift of love can only be known, received, and experienced through a humble heart.

A humble heart is one that can recognize its desperate spiritual state and need of salvation, which results in repentance, and turning to Jesus Christ. It is at this point that God is able to reveal to you how much He loves you, "But God demonstrates his own love for us in this: While we were still sinners, Christ died for us," (Romans 5:8). What allows us to receive and experience God's love is when we humbly acknowledge our sinful state and desperate need of God for salvation and turn to Christ in repentance and faith.[120] It is then that the love of God will be poured out into our hearts through the Holy Spirit.

---

[119] 1 Corinthians 15:1-5
[120] Romans 5:5

HOW TO EXPRESS IT

This brings us to our final point. How do we, as believers in Christ and children of God, express God's love? First of all, we accept that this love belongs to God; therefore, it should be expressed towards Him first.[121] God commanded us to love Him with all our heart, soul, and mind. This means that we are to love Him with our entire being. Jesus Christ demonstrated this in His faithfulness and obedience to God. That faithfulness and obedience called Him to suffer and sacrifice for our sins and salvation. Everything He did, said, thought, and desired was an expression of His love for the Father and for us.[122]

Like Jesus, God has called us to love Him with all of our heart, soul, and mind. The *heart* is the seat of our desires and emotions. It is connected to the mind and the will of man.[123] To love God with all of your heart means to trust Him with your desires and emotions. Instead of acting on what you desire and feel, align your desires with His and trust your feelings to Him.

The *soul* is the entire being of a person. Specifically, it is the will of man. Many times, we deny God's control over our lives, situations, and circumstances because we like to be in control. To love God with all of our soul means to surrender completely to His will and allow Him to rule over every area of our lives.

---

[121] Matthew 22:37; 1 John 4:19
[122] John 10:17-18; Luke 2:49; John 8:29
[123] Holman Illustrated Bible Dictionary

The *mind* is where everything begins for us. What the mind thinks on influences the heart and moves the soul. To love God with our entire mind is to acknowledge Him in all of our ways. It is to align our thoughts with His word and promises.[124]

We were also commanded to love our neighbors as we love ourselves and our fellow brethren as Jesus has loved us.[125] These are two distinct expressions of love. The command to love as we love our self applies to the entire world around us, not just our Christian brothers and sisters. It means doing for others what you would want them to do for you.[126] This means that all of the good you wish for people to do for you, should be offered by you to everyone that you encounter, regardless of who they are, how they treat you, what they do, or what they do not deserve. Jesus made this very clear to us.[127]

In Romans 12:17-21 we are told: " Recompense to no man evil for evil. Provide things honest in the sight of all men. If it be possible, as much as lieth in you, live peaceably with all men. Dearly beloved, avenge not yourselves, but rather give place unto wrath: for it is written, 'Vengeance is mine; I will repay, saith the Lord.' Therefore, if thine enemy hunger, feed him; if he thirsts, give him to drink for in doing so thou shalt heap coals of fire on his head. Be not overcome of evil, but overcome evil with good."

This does not mean that we must love people on their terms. It does not mean that if someone says to you, "If you love me do this for me," you must do it because God said to love them. Instead, it means that you should be good, prayerful,

---

[124] Proverbs 3:5-6; John 14:21-24; Romans 12:1-2
[125] Matthew 22:39; John 15:12-13
[126] Matthew 7:12
[127] Matthew 5:43-44

kind, forgiving, compassionate, merciful, gracious, truthful, helpful, protective, considerate, genuine, and faithful towards them because these are all of the good things you would like to enjoy from others.

Lastly, our Lord commanded us to love one another as He loved us. The love we should express to our fellow brother/sisters comes with the responsibility of teaching, correcting, and warning. It also comes with discipline, encouragement, and admonishing. This love includes the love mentioned above as well. We must be prayerful, kind, forgiving, compassionate, merciful, gracious, truthful, helpful, protective, considerate, genuine, and faithful toward them.

CONCLUSION

God's love is the aim of Christian living because it is the way to please, honor, and glorify Him. We are able to accomplish this through the expression and service of love to God first and those within our realm of influence. What is love then? Love is:

Sacrificial
Suffering
Selfless
Unconditional
Longsuffering
Kind
Humble
Honorable
Enduring
Forgiving
Protective

True
Faithful
Hopeful
Consistent
Merciful
Gracious

Q & A on LOVE

1. What do you know about love? (Explain).
2. Do you believe that you have ever experienced love? (Explain).
3. Do you believe that you have truly loved someone before? (Explain).
4. What is selfish love? (Explain in your own words).
5. Have you ever experienced selfish love or expressed it to others? (Explain).
6. What Is counterfeit love? (Explain in your own words).
7. Have you ever experienced counterfeit love or expressed it to others? (Explain).
8. What is true love?
9. Do you agree or disagree with the description of love in 1 Corinthians 13:4-8? (Explain).
10. Have you ever experienced true love or expressed it to others? (Explain).
11. Where can you find true love?
12. Do you believe true love can be found elsewhere? (Explain where and why).
13. How can one looking for true love find it and experience it?
14. How can we express true love to God? (Explain).
15. If someone asked you, "What is true love," how will you answer them? (Explain).

_____

_____

FINAL CHAPTER

You have finished the ten chapters offered to you in this book. As a reminder of what they are offered to you for, I would like for you to look at these subjects as elements of a foundation rather than just some principles to live by. These are principles for every believer in Christ who claims to believe that Jesus is their Lord and Savior. Together, they make up the foundation one needs to stand in the faith.

When the storms of life come crashing down on me, it is very important that I am rooted in Christ and established in the faith. If I am not rooted and established in the faith when the storm comes, I can be overcome by it rather than overcoming it. My response to the storm will reveal what it is that I rely on the most to get me through the toughest things in life. That response will reveal whether I walk in faith or have no faith.

The principles given to you in this book can help you with how you respond to the storms we face in life. Understanding what hell is and that Jesus Christ delivered me from it, allows me to look at the worst of the things I face in life as something I can get through when I recognize that hell is far worse than anything I can experience in life.

Understanding the seriousness of hell, such as the fact that it is the worst place for anyone to end up in, gives me an appreciation towards God that not only strengthens me in the moment, but also encourages me to trust Him through any trial. I am reminded of how much He cared for me, so much so that He gave His life to deliver me from the penalty of my sin. In other words, when I am facing hardships and difficulties, this understanding increases my faith in Him and encourages me to stand strong and trust Him to deliver me. I am reminded that as He delivered me from hell, He will deliver me from anything.

The principal of repentance reminds me that I have turned away from the lifestyle that I used to live. I am reminded that I have made a decision to turn away from sin and commit my life to Jesus Christ. Understanding that this is what repentance means allows me to learn to take on God's viewpoint on sin so that in the midst of temptation, I am encouraged to say no to my flesh and say yes to God.

When I made the decision to repent, I made the decision to serve God. I had decided to accept this new life He offered me and live it in a manner that pleases, honors, and glorifies Him. Thus, as I stand on this foundation, come what may, I am reminded and encouraged to do what honors, glorifies, and pleases Him.

The principle of salvation has allowed me to understand that I have been saved from hell and I am expected to grow in spiritual maturity and closer to God. I am reminded that I have been born again and am expected to grow into the likeness of God. I am reminded that the gift of salvation is not only deliverance from hell and eternity in heaven, but also the gift of a new life and restored relationship with God the Father.

Therefore, I am expected to grow in these two aspects of salvation. He saved me so that I can spend eternity with Him in heaven, so as I remain on earth, I ought to be demonstrating to Him how much I want to know and grow closer to Him. I have His life and spirit in me, which reminds me that when I die, I will return to Him. As I stand on this principle, I can focus on what is truly important. As I live in this world, I am reminded that God is #1 and those He died for are #2. Thus, drawing closer to Him and becoming Christ like is of the utmost importance to me.

The principle of faith is one that means more than I can express. It related to everything I am, do, think, desire, go through, enjoy, hope for, and expect to obtain in the future. As I stand on this principle, I am encouraged to examine myself to be sure that I am living and walking by faith. In other words, whatever I am getting ready to choose or decide to do I ask myself, "Am I trusting God with it?" I can't please Him unless I trust Him to guide me in my choices and decisions. This is a challenge for me every day. My faith in God is tested every day.

I am constantly tested to see if I will depend on Him or myself for guidance, instruction, provision, etc. The more I trust Him, the more I increase in faith. Therefore, when I am tempted to decided for myself and act like I know better than

He does, this principle encourages me to seek God and trust in Him only.

Hope is a principle that refocuses my attention on things above when I get distracted by things below. When I am focused on things that are not of God, this principle reminds me to get back on track. In this life, I have faced challenges that have caused me at times to focus on the wrong things. Hope reminds me that I am not of this world. It reminds me that I am a foreigner in this world and that I am here temporarily until my Lord Jesus picks me up.

This reminder is very important to me because it reminds me that I have gone all in on the day that the Lord will pick me up and encourages me to focus on the reason I am in the world until that day comes. I am reminded that I am in this world to be a blessing, not just to enjoy blessings. I am also reminded not to allow myself to become a slave to the blessings I can enjoy in this world and forget that I am a servant of God.

Grace reminds me that I have all the help I need in the hands of my heavenly Father. I am reminded that I do not have to worry about food, clothing, or shelter because my Father knows that I need them and will provide them for me. I am reminded, as I stand on this principle, that I do not have to give my life to make money in order to make provision of these things for myself, because my Father in heaven has what I need already in store for me. As long as I ask, seek, and knock for it, I will obtain it. This encourages me to rely on Him more than people, places, and things.

Furthermore, on a spiritual level, if I need forgiveness, love, joy, peace, self-control, guidance, protection, strength, etc., I know that He has it in store for me also. In other words, the principle of grace reminds me that He has everything that I need. This principle also humbles me because it reminds me of how much I need God. This need encourages me to be who He is for me to others, because just as I need grace every day, so does everyone else.

The principle of truth keeps me from being misled, misguided, led astray, deceived, manipulated, and/or placed in harms way. First of all, I am reminded that the truth comes from God. Whatever people say, think, or feel about me is not what I ought to allow to influence my choices and decisions in life. If the words or actions of others upset me, hurt me, or provoke me to anger, I am reminded to hear what God said on that matter before acting on it. As I stand on this principle, I am reminded that the truth of God can set me free of all evil.

I am reminded that the truth is my light, clarity, and life. I am also reminded that it is my defense that brings down anything that attempts to exalt itself above the knowledge of God. The truth then activates my faith in God.

As I stand upon the principle of prayer, I am reminded that I have a direct "phone line" which allows me to communicate what is going on with me and in the world to my Father in heaven. I am reminded that my heavenly Father is always expecting my call. I am reminded that there is no small matter or great enough problem that I cannot bring to him in prayer. I am also reminded that my heavenly Father really wants me to rely on Him. I am reminded that He really wants to know me. Furthermore, prayer confirms to me how much the life in me depends upon my communication with God. Every time I feel powerless, I am reminded that prayer keeps me connected to my source of power.

Everything I need is just a call away, so when I am in need, I know that I only have to ask my Father and He will provide.

The more I grow in my prayer life the more I grow in my spiritual life. If or when I desire to bring Heaven down on earth, prayer is the way.

The principle of forgiveness reminds me of how much I need it from my Father in heaven, which keeps me humble in cases where someone needs it from me. It is a reminder of how much I desire to remain in connection with my Father in heaven when I am wronged by another. I am reminded to respond to someone's insults, persecution, dishonesty, and evil acts with forgiveness, because this is how God would respond to me.

I am reminded of my own weaknesses, faults, and errors. As I stand on this principal, I am encouraged to accept people with all of their weaknesses, faults, and errors so that when they appear, I am quick to forgive, responding in compassion, grace, longsuffering, and love instead of revenge. This principal reminds me that my Lord Jesus Christ died for me, so that I may be forgiven.

Finally, the principal of love is everything to me. It is proof that I know God and that I am His child. As I express love to others, I am testifying, in action, that I have been delivered from hell. I have repented, I am saved, I have faith, I have hope, I am growing in grace, I live by truth, I do commune with God, I am forgiven, and I am an expression of God's love.

To be an expression of God's love is my purpose. When I struggle with the concept of love, God reminds me, "The Lord is compassionate and gracious, slow to anger and abounding in love." In other words, He reminds me of who He is towards me, and this is why I ought to love my enemy, neighbor, and others. This principal is the power of God inside of me for all of those who have not known Him or tasted of His goodness.

May this foundation help you stand and keep you standing in the faith, regardless of the storms you face in life. I know it has allowed me to experience God's love, peace, and joy even in the stormy weather. May you experience the same and more. May God bless you. In Jesus' name.

DEDICATIONS

First and foremost, I want to say that it if wasn't for God, my heavenly Father, I would not have been able to write or put this powerful book together. Therefore, I want to dedicate this work to my Lord and Savior Jesus the Christ. You are the rock of my life. You have become my foundation. If it weren't for the knowledge of You, I would never have been able to offer the world this great wisdom and understanding of what a firm foundation in the believer's life can look like or consist of. I pray that this work brings You much honor and glory, as only You deserve.

With that said, I also wish to dedicate this book to those I have hurt in anyway. I especially dedicate this book to the family of Aaron McCrea, who is no longer with us or his family due to gun violence and the many evil influences that corrupt the minds and hearts of people like myself. I am so sorry that your beloved lost his life at my hands. I am sorry that I did not know then what I know now. I pray that someday you can find peace.

I know that there is not much I can say to convince you that I am no longer that same person who took the life of your beloved, but I plan to prove this to you by my service to my Lord Jesus. This book is a demonstration to you of what I stand for. I am deeply remorseful for the pain and grief I have caused you. As long as I live, I will always be reminded that there is a family in this world whose lives I have forever changed and painfully impacted. I can only hope that the Lord who transformed my life can also comfort your hearts and fill them with the love that I have stolen from you.

To my family, who I have selfishly left behind and hurt as well, I want to dedicate this book to you. I hope to one day be able to help you lay down this foundation in your lives as it has been laid out in my life. I know that you have experienced so much upset, failure, and disappointment in your lives due to the lack of trustworthy/reliable foundations that can guide you in the choices and decisions you make for your future.

This book is here to help you correct what has been wrong in our lives for so long. I know you love me. I know life is difficult. I understand that things get in our way. However, I hope you can take the time you need to be better equipped when you have to confront your future obstacles. I love you.

For all of you who have purchased this book, I want to say that this book is also dedicated to you. I pray that you are able to benefit from this work as much as I have. I look forward to working with you in the near future.

ABOUT THE AUTHOR

To some, life deals them a good hand where they, as children, are protected from the worst things in life and only exposed to the things that will allow them to grow into the best human beings that they can be. However, for others, like myself, life deals them a bad hand, where no protection is provided from the worst possible situations that they can experience in life.

That exposure forces them to grow into a product of their enviornment. This was my case.

I was born and raised in New Haven, Connecticut. My neighborhood was called, "The Hill." I had moved a lot in The Hill. Every block that I had lived on was a block with a lot of drugs and other criminal activity. There were drug dealers, drug addicts, gang bangers, and prostitutes everywhere that I went. I was always witnessing fights, domestic violence, drug abuse, alcoholics, and other things that were going on in my surroundings or neighborhood.

People would steal cars to get from point A to point B, drug addicts would rent their cars for some drugs to local drug dealers, and women would prostitute themselves to get their next fix. Sirens and shootings were a regular thing. Unless you heard a window crash or saw someone near you drop to the ground, you did not jump at the sound of a shot fired. You simply looked around to see where it was coming from.

Sirens from police cars or ambulances were ignored completely until they showed up beside you, in front of your house, or at a friend's place. There were so many teenage mothers around us with father issues. They hung around my friends and me, looking for attention and love. We did not have to get to know them to have sex with them.

My parents were drug addicts. In addition to that, my father was a gang banger and a drug dealer. He spent most of my childhood in prison or on the streets, so I never had an opportunity to build a relationship with him. As a child, I remember he hit me whenever I snitched on him to my mother or my sister. That is how I learned not to snitch. He also taught me that I can always find a job selling drugs or that I could have a family by joining a gang.

I guess the bad experiences I had with my family were enough for me not to go in search of another. My mother never had a job, so whenever my father went to prison, she was left to support three kids on welfare. This would be hard for any single parent with no job, is on welfare, and also has a bad drug addiction. She tried though. I remember sleeping in shelters, the homes of drug addicts, the homes of strangers, the homes of relatives, and other places.

I remember living in this house that had almost thirty rooms for rent in it. Every room was occupied by a drug addict. My mother was brought there by this guy she was dating at the time who was renting the first two rooms at the entrance of the house. My sister and I slept in one room while they slept in the other.

In this one house, I witnessed a lot. The drug traffic was insane. All of the money the drug addicts spent there on drugs went to my mother's boyfriend. They brought in stolen goods and performed sexual acts for their drugs. I witnessed it all. I also observed people selling drugs, fighting, stabbings, shootings, overdoses, and raids while I lived there. This was a world within the world.

While all of this was going on, I was in seventh grade. My middle school was just across the street, and I could not attend school because I had no clean clothing most of the time. My mother could not afford to buy me new clothing. Her boyfriend was not going to spend his money on me, so I did not go to school. At that time, the friends I went to school with were going through similar circumstances, so they had begun hustling crack for older drug dealers on their block. I was not from their block yet, so I could not deal for them. They also said I looked too young to be out there.

Before my mother left this guy, I found my own way at twelve years old or so. I began selling drugs to provide for myself. I began selling ten-dollar bags of heroin on a street named Congress Avenue, where another one of my friends from school sold his drugs. I started with fifty dollars and doubled it. I made a thousand dollars one night and could not stop selling drugs after that.

It felt really good to provide for myself. Money at the time meant food, clothing, and shelter. When my mother's boyfriend got us an apartment, on the same block my friends were selling crack on, my mother ended her relationship with him. She found out that I was selling drugs when she saw all of the new clothes I brought into the house. She cheered me on, though she was not happy that I was selling drugs. She was glad that I did not have to suffer from our impoverished conditions anymore, so she encouraged me to get that money.

We were living on a street called Liberty Street in an apartment building when my father had been released from prison into a halfway house. He was sneaking over to our apartment to see my mother. This was a violation of his conditions of release, so when he was caught, he was returned to prison. Around the same time, the Department of Child Services was riding around our neighborhood kidnapping my friends and making them disappear.

One of my friends lived across the street from me. His mother had a bad addiction to heroin. D.C.F found out about her situation and raided his home looking for him. They found enough drug paraphernalia to take him into their custody. He managed to escape hours later. When he returned to us, he told us that he had jumped out of their car while it was moving and made his escape.

I feared that I was next because my mother had lost her apartment without telling me that she needed money to pay the rent. She must have been too ashamed to ask me for help. This forced her to go to D.C.F. for "help" but the only "help" they were willing to offer was to take my sister and me into their custody, so we ran from them.

I remember being on my own after that. I had to survive. The only way that I knew how to do this was to sell drugs. While in the streets, I learned some principles, values, and lessons that guided my choices and decisions. I learned that in order to continue to sell drugs in the hood, I had to make sure: 1.) Not to SNITCH, 2.) Not to step on anyone else's toes, 3.) Be ready to step up for my own or ride for my own, 4.) Keep it real, 5.) Earn my respect, 6.) Be loyal and 7.) Show love to my people.

I had to develop a reputation in order for people in the hood to respect me. I was not a shooter, but if someone disrespected me, it was a challenge. I had to decide to let it go or to make an example of that person. The cost of such a decision is the only thing that mattered at the time because depending on who found out in the hood, that one act of disrespect could be the reason that you became a target.

If people in the hood find out that you are not willing to defend yourself, you will become a victim, especially if you sell drugs. Snitching carried a different type of consequence in the hood. Some people will kill you for that. Others who do not want to risk their lives will just extort you every time they see you.

I lived by these principles. I earned the title of a "real nigga" in the hood. My values were love, loyalty, and respect. However, these values meant something totally different to me and those who I grew up with. For example, loyalty means that you stuck to these principles and had your friends' backs, no matter what. Right or wrong, you had to "ride" for your people. Love meant that I do for you, and you do for me. If I have it, so do you.

Respect came from the recognition that you made yourself a man who lives by the combination of these principles and values in addition to putting in the kind of "work" expected of you when situations got difficult. These values held a little more meaning to them, but this is what they stand for.

D.C.F. took me off the streets by surprise. I can't really remember exactly how it all went down. I just remember my mother asked me to accompany her to an office they had in the Yale area right next to a highway ramp. I knew that she was going to them for assistance, but I already had experienced some funny business with them that had me cautious about the kind of "assistance" they wanted to lend to my mother.

Remember what I shared earlier with you? This is what happened. Nearly a year earlier, my mother had lost her apartment and taken us with her to the D.C.F. central office in New Haven. As we waited for her to come out of the meeting, she was having with them, she had suddenly burst out of their office into the waiting room that we were in and had screamed at us to run. They were trying to take us from her. That day, we got away and had been in the streets ever since.

It was sometime after this that we ended up at D.C.F. looking for some help again. At this time, I was heavily involved in the streets. I told her that I was going to be all right, but she refused to let me fend for myself. Long story short, it was a setup. They took us away from my mother and placed us in their custody. All that I remember after that is that they put me into a mental hospital for running away from them that day.

I ran across the highway to the "Jungle," which is a housing complex/project that I used to hang out in with my friends.

For some reason, they had two agents waiting for me there. When I arrived, they snatched me up and took me with them. They put me in a mental hospital for six to eight months and labeled me suicidal.

The things that I witnessed in the mental hospital were traumatizing. There were so many kids acting out and trying to kill themselves in there. I saw the staff slam and restrain anyone who acted out or refused to take their medication. The staff would pull the kids' pants down and would stick needles full of drugs into their bottoms to sedate them. The staff would leave the kids on four-point restraints until they calmed down and became obedient. After witnessing this, I took the "depression" medication they gave to me every day.

I was released to a group home for boys in Westport Connecticut after they determined that nothing was wrong with me. There was no school, no form of education, no activities, just a bunch of orphan boys in a mini-mansion living together because D.C.F. had placed all of us there. We were sometimes brought to the beach or to places where we could shop with the state voucher that was given to us. Anything to get out of the house. For whatever reason, this place was closed down and I was placed in a group home in my hometown of New Haven.

At this group home, I had to fight off bullies and protect myself and my belongings. This was not difficult for me because of what I had learned in the streets. The moment I was given the opportunity to escape and stay with a relative, I did. The relative was my oldest sister, who at the time, was living with her husband's family. At the time there was about 10 people living there, so I did not plan to stay there long. I had developed an independent mentality at a very young age, so

I did not like the idea or feeling of waiting for others to take care of my needs.

While living with them, I had started to visit my friends, who were glad to see me again as they had not seen me in two years because of D.C.F. I got back onto my feet quickly. My friend was making a lot of money selling crack on Kimberly Avenue in my neighborhood. I joined him and we began selling our drugs off of a cell phone and partnered up. I was staying at another friend's house for the time being until I was able to get an addict to rent me a hotel room every week.

I ended up getting caught with a bunch of drugs in this hotel when I made the mistake of serving a client of mine at the hotel. The addict showed up in a huge 18-wheeler truck and parked it right at the window of my room. All of the light from the truck lit up my room and all of my friends and I thought there was some U.F.O outside. I tried to rush the client out of the area, but it was too late.

The hotel was under surveillance by the police. They found out where I was and raided my room. We got caught with seventy-two bags of crack and two ounces of untouched crack. I say "we" because my friends were with me that day.

Before I had been caught by the police, I had been dealing with my older cousin. He was selling grade A weed at the time. He wanted me to be his partner, but he was not making enough money at the time for me to partner up with him. I just helped him as best as I could. He had just come out of prison and was on probation. All we used to do was hang out most of the time.

I was still partnered up with my friend. I had a girlfriend and a few side things I messed around with. My girlfriend had her own car, so I kind of used her for that purpose. She was really a good one though. I had introduced her to my world and broke her heart in the process. Her mistake was trusting me with her heart.

My first time being locked up did not teach me anything. I left prison hating the guards and how they treated prisoners. I also left prison thinking that I would be able to do the wrong things the right way. This was all I spoke of with the other prisoners. Getting money was a hot topic in prison. We had dreams of becoming the next Scar Face, King of New Haven, or the person our favorite rappers rapped about, selling drugs was the way to make those dreams come true, I thought

I was let off easy the first time. The court agreed to send me to an inpatient program for six months and then they would determine whether or not to release me based on my good behavior. My girlfriend came to visit me with my cousin one day at the program. My cousin informed me that he was selling kilos of coke. This means that he had made it to the big leagues in the drug game.

He asked me to be his partner when I came out of the program and I quickly agreed. Before I completed the program, I ran away from it and joined him. The things that he introduced me to were not for a 16-year-old. He took me to strip clubs, nightclubs, and other scenes that made me feel grown. I was proud that someone as young as me was able to do these things.

We shared women, we went on shopping sprees and drove around the neighborhood rubbing our success in everyone's faces. The crowd that he brought me around was an older one and they called us Diddy and Cuban after the rapper's Puff Daddy and Cuban Link. I was known by the bigger drug dealers because of him. They told me that they liked me more than my cousin because of the way that I carried myself around them.

Everyone knew how young I was, but they understood my situation, so they overlooked it. At sixteen years old, I was supplying the neighborhood with the crack that fed the beast inside my mother and destroyed her life. I did not care though. All I cared about was the "all mighty dollars." Working 9-5 at a job was not for me, so I thought. My sister tried it with me when I lived with her and my brother-in-law. It got me a few nice things, but it could not provide what I wanted. I wanted to be a "baller."

As I hustled with my cousin, I would always visit my friends who were struggling like I was, trying to make ends meet. I came by regularly to visit them in the projects, (The Jungle). It was usually my friend Roger, Carlito, and Chucky. There were others, but these were the ones I closely related to and grew up with. Our life circumstances were almost identical. This is what brought us together and why we were so close. I showed them love and they showed me love. We looked out for each other, even to this day, except for Carlito, who is no longer with us. Shout out to them, I love ya'll.

Roger, Carlito, and I had caught our first case together in that hotel that I told you about. Since then, we had become stuck in the revolving door that leads to the prison system. Other friends of ours were Hec, Kanky, Tili, Los, and Josue. I had other friends on Kimberly Avenue as well, like Pete, Will, Train-B, and others, but these guys were the guys I hung out with on the regular, with the exception of Pete and Will.

I introduced them to you because we lived by that code: Loyalty, Love, Respect. Every time we came out of prison and fell onto hard times, or got into some trouble, we would stand in the gap for each other the only way that we knew how to.

My life consisted of selling drugs, smoking weed, drinking, partying, watching out for the police, buying nice things, sleeping around with random women, and defending my reputation and possessions. We are taught very early in the game that if you hustle, you better look out for the stick-up kids. I was first to be robbed at gun point in broad day light. They made off with a couple of hundred dollars, some weed, and my car.

My cousin/partner was the next one to be robbed at gun point in broad day light. This was personal though. He was robbed by his own people. It was a member of the same gang that my cousin was a part of. This did something to me that I cannot identify. All that I know is that I began to have this desire to kill one of the people who robbed us. I felt like we were targets in the neighborhood. I felt like people thought they can get away with taking from us and not have to worry about any consequences. I lived paranoid.

My cousin and I went on a shopping spree for guns after that. We bought Glock-45s and Glock—9s with beams in them. We bought Smith and Wesson 9mm, 357 bull dogs, Street Sweepers, SK rifles, and bullet proof vests. I was under the impression that we were going to get revenge and make a big statement to everyone who thought they could get away with robbing us.

There were times that people who bought crack from us would sit in the passenger seat of my cousin's car and not know that I was in the back seat aiming a fully loaded Glock-9 to the back of their head, ready to shoot if they tried anything stupid.

Eventually, I had to separate myself from my cousin because he started to show how disloyal he was when my father came out of prison. He basically gave my father my part of the business and excluded me. I wanted to kill them both for the betrayal, but I could not commit such a heartless act. I took this very personally because before my father had showed up, we ran into the guy who had robbed my cousin. I was going to shoot the guy; he had talked me out of doing anything to the dude. I could not deal with him anymore, so I cut him off and tried to make it on my own again.

So many things happened during this time, between my cousin, father, and I, that had me on the brink of losing it. One day, I showed up at the apartment we all shared and caught them both with a different girl that I was sleeping with. After that, my cousin slept with this girl that I had been engaged to. He made sure he took the guns and hid them from me. Then he told the gun connection we had not to sell me anything because I would kill someone. These guys had crossed so many lines with me that they wouldn't have crossed with others in the hood because they feared someone else would probably kill them, but I could not do it because they were family.

To be done with all of the stress that I held on to, I turned myself into the police department and decided to get my warrant over and done with. I had a girlfriend who was pregnant. I did not want to be on the run from the police with a kid, so I went in. I turned myself into the police department and was sentenced to two years. I would only serve half of that.

The year I was locked up, I ended up getting into many fights. One was with an older guy that owed my friend money. My friend did not want to fight him, so I did. Then, while in solitary confinement, I got into another fight with one of the guys that had robbed me in the streets. As soon as I saw him, I wailed on him. This was called "on site fights." It was when you saw someone who did something wrong to you or violated you in some type of way, and the first thing you did was get your pay back.

People in the hood handle a lot of their problems this way. This is why you hear of so many shootings and murders. It is because the person who was shot or killed did something to violate that person who shot and killed them. It was a respect thing. The point you were making to the person and the people around at the time was noticeably clear, anyone who dares to violate can expect the same thing and these are the rules that you play by.

Anyway, I got into another fight while I was in solitary confinement on another court trip. To be clear, I was still going to court and had not been sentenced yet. This made the D.O.C send me to a super max prison that was high security. They labeled me a threat to the inmate population. For eight months, I was forced to shower with my hands cuffed and shackled around my ankles.

I was allowed out of my 6 by 9 cell for an hour a day. I had to place a request with the time, date, and person I wanted to call for a phone call. I was not allowed contact visits from anyone, not even my family. The only outside air that I was allowed to breath was in a caged space that was polluted with toxins that came out of a nearby exhaust system.

By the time that I was released back into the regular prison population, it was time for me to be released back into society. I did not receive any form of psychological treatment after this experience. For eight or so months, I was cut off from everything that reminded me that I was human. Within the blink of an eye, I was released back into society. I had no rehabilitative treatment or encouragement to personally develop myself.

I had not learned why I thought the way that I thought, believed what I believed, or perceived things the way that I did. I was not aware of any negative influences in my life that contributed to so many bad experiences and outcomes. All I was subjected to was torture for the past eight months, and now I was back in the same streets and in the same neighborhood that claimed my soul.

This is how it usually was whenever I was incarcerated. I did not receive any correction or treatment. I was just given time for the crime that I committed and then, after serving that time, released back into the same neighborhood that remained infested with crime. This time was different. I had suffered more than I knew. The damage that I suffered mentally and emotionally in my conditions of confinement made me so angry that I knew I could explode at any given time.

In addition to all of this, my girlfriend, who was pregnant before I turned myself in, had an abortion while I was in. Being there for her while she was pregnant was important to me but being there for the baby when he or she was born was even more important, so this had encouraged me to turn myself in and begin a new life with her when I was released. When I found out that she had an abortion, I began to act out, giving rise to all of the fights I had.

When I was released, I felt like I had suffered all of this for nothing, so there was a lot of resentment, anger, and rage built up inside. I was also reminded every day of my father and cousins' betrayal, and this added to the rage that I felt.

Despite how I felt upon release, I still wanted to do things the right way this time. I did not want to go back to prison. I was living with my older sister and her husband. I had a few dollars that I used to buy some clothing and a car. I had my driver's license and registered my car under my own name to build my credit and then I got a job at the New Haven Register. It was only paying me $400 every two weeks, but I did not care. I would keep working there until I obtained a better job.

I did not want to go back to prison. However, I did not have my High School diploma or G.E.D. and I was a convicted felon. These things, coupled with my lack of effective communication skills worked against me every time I applied for a job. Not even McDonald's wanted to give me a job.

My friends, Roger, Carlito, and Will came by to see me the minute they found out that I was released. They offered me help, but the kind of help they were offering was the type that could get me back in prison, so I was not in a rush to accept it. For the time being, I declined and stuck with this new struggle. I was still messing around with different girls and partying when I got the chance.

The main ones that I was hanging out with during this time was my friend Carlito and Will. They would call me every day to pick them up. Together, we would drive around after I came home from work, and we would drink. We would hang out together at some girl's house, then the park, or the projects. My friend Roger had gotten too big to hang out with us.

On September 17, 2006, at 12:30 a.m. my friend Carlito was shot dead in the projects that we hung out in. Just hours before he was killed, we were supposed to go to some party at a night club that we were all invited to. It was my friend Will's sister's birthday party. We had all agreed to attend together. I told them both that I would pick them up at 10 p.m. Carlito was the last to pick up, since it was on the way to the night club.

He was staying with some girl he had gotten pregnant in the projects, so I had told him to be ready at 10 p.m. at the front of the projects entrance on Church Street South. When I arrived, he was nowhere to be found. I called his cell phone and there was no answer, so my friend told me that he was probably busy with his girl. We ended up going to the club without him.

Around 11 p.m., he called me and asked me to pick him up. I refused to leave the club because there was no parking anywhere, so I had parked my car in the rear by the V.I.P parking. We left the club around 1:45 a.m. I dropped my friend Will off at his house and went home myself. My mother woke me up at around 11 a.m. telling me that Will was trying to call me because our friend had been killed.

I immediately jumped out of bed, got dressed, and met Will in the projects. When I arrived, there was a vigil set up in front of the project's big green dumpsters. I saw my friends gathering together at the housing unit of another friend named Primo. Primo was an older guy from the projects that we all respected since we were young. He went partying and hanging out with us from time to time.

I joined them all and asked why the vigil for our friend Carlito was set up at the project's dumpster. They told me that it was where he was killed. I was already guilt tripping because I felt like I could have prevented his death had I just picked him up that night. The fact that he was killed behind a dumpster infuriated me. I felt disrespected for him.

After inquiring, I was told that he was robbed and killed. Some young kid we knew from the projects approached us and told us that he had been present when Carlito was killed. He told us that A-Love had killed him because Carlito would not stop selling crack in the projects. We were all aware that A-Love was trying to take over the drug business in the projects, so we got it.

The kid said that Carlito's dying words to him were, the guy who did it took his chain. The kid said that A-Love's cousin, "King Weezy" and another guy did it for A-Love. Moments later, one of A-Love's close friends approached us saying that A-Love was the one who had killed him and that the only reason he was telling us was because he was friends with Carlito as well. He did not like the way that this all went down.

After he left, my friend showed up with two guns. To get revenge for Carlito's death. The only issue was that no one wanted to step up, so me and another friend each took a gun and agreed to honor Carlito's name. Although the reason my friend was killed was not clear to us, we were sure that we knew who did it because that kid and A-Love's friend had good credibility in the projects.

We were hanging out a while with each other grieving the loss of our friend when we saw A-Love on a bike. He rode right past us, passing the vigil as if nothing had happened. I watched him as he passed my friends vigil, and he did not even look at it. I knew about A-Love. Although I did not have a personal relationship with him, I knew that he was not someone you should mess around with unless you were willing to die.

We had heard about some other guy he had killed and had gotten away with it. He had supposedly taken off to Atlanta after, which was why he left his business in the projects behind. To be honest, I was filled with so much rage inside that I knew if I saw him, I would do something. Unfortunately for him, I saw him, and what I saw did not help his situation.

My friend and I followed him to Church Street South where he was speaking to a crack addict, and we fired. I let off every shot in the gun at him. I completely blacked out. When I came to my senses, I heard my friend telling me to run, so I ran with him. I was full of adrenaline and fear at the same time. It was broad day light and about eighty degrees outside. I even forgot that I had my car parked right where I had shot A-Love. I just ran right past it following my friend to another friend's house. I dropped the gun off there, changed my clothing and left with another friend who we called to pick us up.

What I had done started to dawn on me later on after it was all done. I could not believe that I had done this. It was not real to me, and I thought that I had done the right thing. Someone had killed my friend, so I killed him. An eye for an eye is what we call it. It was code in the streets. We could not call the police because of the life we lived. I could not believe that I had done it though.

I could see my life being taken away from me very soon. I knew it was just a matter of time before someone decided to kill me in retaliation or tell the police on me. Many people told on me. In addition to that, my co-defendant made up a story and told the police that Primo paid me $15,000 to kill A-Love and gave me two guns to do it. The police ended up getting some other people to write statements against me and told the court that they either saw me do it or had seen me with the guns that did it.

I tried to throw them off my trail when they picked me up, by telling them that people might be confusing me with my cousin and told them that the only person I knew by the name "Bebe" was this guy named Julio that I went to school with. I told them that he was the one who did it. I thought that if I gave them another suspect or two, they would stop looking at me and my co-defendant and turn their focus on them. My co-defendant blew the whole thing, and they were able to build a case on us.

I was only in the streets for two weeks after coming home from prison before this happened. Two weeks after the incident, I was back in prison. I went to trial expecting that I would win the case against me because my co-defendant told me that he would not take the stand against me. I also had a good defense of third party culpability, because some guy was running around the hood claiming that he did the crime.

God had different plans for me though. I did not believe in God at the time, He was heavily involved in my situation at this time. He knew that in my heart I was thinking that if I beat this murder I would use it as a badge of honor and who knows what other things I would have done to destroy my neighborhood. Anyone who got away with killing someone earned the ultimate level of respect in the hood.

For me, that meant that I would be able to make a lot of money without the worry of anyone trying me or challenging me for it. At least that was what I was looking forward to. However, it did not work out that way for me. Instead, I lost the trial and was sentenced to fifty years in prison. I could have gotten off easier than that, when the prosecutor offered me ten years for a plea bargain, but I did not take it.

I wanted to beat this case, instead, I beat myself.

For the first seven years of my sentence, I was bitter, angry, and rebellious. I was mad that all of my friends had left me for dead the minute that I was charged and incarcerated. No one got me a lawyer, sent me money for my commissary, or made sure that my mother was all right. They just left me for dead. Then my family left me for dead. I felt as if I had no one. Then I found out as I was fighting my case that my friend Carlito was killed because he had snitched on A-Love about a shooting he did.

A-Love had done time for the shooting because of Carlito and vowed that he would get revenge for that, so he did. When I found this out I felt like I had been deceived. I found out that I was the only one who did not know this before shooting A-Love. Not only had my friends left me for dead in this situation that I was in, but they also had withheld information from me. I believe that this information would have changed my mind concerning the entire situation.

I would not have done anything to A-Love had I known this, but I did not, so I did. I believed in the "Code." No snitching was #1. He did what he was supposed to do in the hood. We all know that. In my messed-up way of thinking, I thought, two real niggas lost their lives that day. The ones who believed in the code and would ride out for it, me, and A-Love.

I had no hope left inside of me. I felt abandoned, betrayed, deceived, misled, taken advantage of, and left for dead. Every time I acted out in defiance of the D.O.C. (Department of Corrections) rules and regulations, I was placed in isolative confinement. There, I would reflect on what I had done.

I kept getting into trouble because I was angry. I blamed everyone and everything for all of my past failures, upsets, and disappointments. It was easier for me not to think of my crime because I already felt like I did wrong for killing A-Love under the belief that it was "unjust" in hood terms.

My last trip to isolative confinement did it for me. I was really considering killing myself, but my mother came to mind. I thought of a conversation that I had had with her over the phone before I was placed in solitary confinement. My sister had bought a dog and named it Macho, my nick name. When it died, she called my mother hysterical and in tears, telling her that Macho had died.

My mom had immediately thought that it was me and lost it. Crazy right? She broke her cell phone in grief so my sister could not call her back and tell her that it was not me, but her dog. My mother told my grandmother, who lived upstairs at the time, and she lost it. My sister was able to contact my grandmother and inform them that it was her dog that she was talking about, and everyone settled down.

It was funny at the time, but as I thought about suicide, I remembered that and could not cause that kind of grief on my family. Then I thought about what I learned from my grandmother when I was young, how that anyone who killed themselves went to hell and anyone that killed someone went to hell as well. I had never thought about the consequences of my decision before this day.

It was 2011. I thought to myself, "if what grandma taught me is true, then I better be finding the way to escape from hell." As I thought about this, I also began thinking that God's forgiveness was not the only forgiveness I needed. A-Love's family was hurt by me in ways that are indescribable. Despite what I believed, felt, or knew about him, his family loved him like my family loved me.

I thought about how my mother, father, sisters, grandmother, and family would feel towards the person who killed me if I were to be in his shoes. They would have been devastated. They would have wanted my killer dead. They would have hated him. At that moment, I began crying. I finally felt what I did to A-Love's family.

I had been in isolative confinement now for about two weeks. There was no one with me, it was nighttime, and I stood at the narrow window of my cell. I stared at the full moon. I did not know if God was real, I just cried to Him for forgiveness. I begged Him to help the family of A-love forgive me one day. I told Him that I was tired of the direction my life was headed. I asked Him to save me from hell and change my life. I did not want to be the person that I had become anymore. At the same time, I knew that only He had the power to change me, so I asked for it.

A few days after I set the prayer, I was transferred to another prison. I was still in solitary confinement. A week later, I was released back into the general population with a disciplinary report and sanctions. I met this guy named Frankie who I had come to know when I was waiting for my trial in high bond.

Frankie was a man of faith. He believed in God and let everyone know that he did by sharing scriptures with them. When he saw me, he immediately was drawn to me and inquired about my situation and circumstances. I informed him as to what circumstances brought me there with him. He told me that this was not a coincidence, and that God had a plan for me if I believed. I did not know what he meant by that, so I ignored it and continued to do my time as I knew how.

In prison, there are ways to smuggle in and get drugs or other things we wanted. I was always looking for weed to smoke and porn to look at. I am just being honest. Throughout my prison bid, I was known as the guy who had or can get the weed or drugs. I like to make money and find my own way still. In prison, if you sold drugs, you were, "The Man." It was something I still struggled to let go of. Plus, I had to survive because my family and friends left me for dead.

Even though Frankie knew that I was up to no good, he approached me every day with a scripture to read, so I read it. It seemed to me that every scripture that I read and applied in my life confirmed to me that this was where the truth was.

These scriptures told me that if I obeyed them, I could expect a certain outcome.

I tested it to see if it was true and things would turn out exactly as it said. I knew God was trying to speak to my heart, but I did not know what it was that He wanted me to know. This went on for three months, and I told Frankie about it. He asked me if I wanted to go to a church service with him one night, so I went. That night, I heard the preacher say to everyone, "If you are looking for forgiveness, saving from hell, and a change of life, Jesus Christ is the way."

This shocked me to hear because it was what I had asked God for when I was in isolated confinement before I was transferred to this prison. I could not deny the fact that God was actually responding to my prayers through this man. He asked everybody that night that if we desired to accept Jesus Christ as our personal Lord and savior, he and his crew were willing to pray with us and lead us into God's saving grace, so I went for it. This was on November 28, 2012.

Every day after that I began to experience a conviction on nearly everything that I did, said, thought, desired, heard, and especially smoked. My new cell mate was a God-fearing man, which was rare in prison. Every day he did his personal Bible studies and encouraged others to accept Jesus Christ as their personal Lord and Savior. I came to Jesus with more baggage than I can describe. In fact, I was still selling weed in prison when I was saved.

Every day my cell mate did his studies I was next to him smoking weed and offering some to him. He never indulged though, which made me feel really bad. I would ask him while high as a kite if I could have bible study with him. He never denied me the opportunity no matter how high I was. It was amazing. Every time that I read the Bible with him while I was high, it would sober me up fast. I would tell him that God was letting me know that He was not pleased with this.

Weed was the first thing that I let go of. I could not enjoy it anymore. What used to be a delight turned into a disappointment every time that I indulged, so I let it go. I then stopped cursing when I spoke because it felt wrong when I did. The music I listened to made me reminisce about the days that I used to do all kinds of things wrong, so I got rid of all of it.

I then began letting go of people who called themselves friends but were negative influences in my life. The last thing that I got rid of was porn. God began to clean up my life slowly but surely. Every day I studied my bible. The more I studied, the more I got to know him. I desired to change. I began taking a different view of my life. My thinking changed in a major way. I was being educated through the Bible, on all matters of life. This influenced my choices and decisions.

I signed up for school to obtain my G.E.D and got it. I then began to further my education by enrolling in vocational programs. I came across some bumps and hurdles, but I was able to overcome them and not be overcome by them like before. I began going to church service everyday they had it. I obtained a job as a resource center clerk. I served the prison population by ministering to them what God had taught me.

Prison guards recognized the change that God had made in me, and in my life. They started treating me with a lot of respect. I did not break any of the rules or bother anyone. I just stood by myself or did what I could do to help someone in the manner God allowed me to. Things just began to change for me. I was able to experience what success is. I was so used to upsets, failures and disappointments that the consistent success I was experiencing, even on a small level, made me really appreciate what it felt like.

I knew it was God. I had learned to renew my mind (perceptual process) and heart, and it was transforming me and producing good fruit in my life. God allowed me to develop a different perspective of life. Understanding that He gave His only Son to die on a cross, so that people like me can be saved, made me look at the crime that I committed in a different light.

God was trying to save life and I was responsible for taking one from this earth. God had opened my eyes to what was truly important to Him which is human life. He wanted to redeem us and forgive us of all our wrongs, transfer us from death to life, give us a new identity, adopt us into His family, transform us into His image and likeness and bring us into heaven with Him for eternity.

He did not want us to die in our depraved condition or fallen nature and suffer the penalty of our sins. After this revelation, I gave myself to Him for saving and building lives. He wanted me to become an expression of His love in this world and to tell everyone about Jesus and the gift of salvation. He wanted me to help build those people into His followers, so I took on this mission.

I began conducting bible studies in prison. I gathered together men who wanted to be saved and transformed into small groups and led them into salvation. I then began focusing on building them up into disciples. I helped them with their identity in Christ and relationship with the Father until they were transformed. In the resource center, I did the same thing. However, since I could not hold a bible study there, I started a correspondence thing with many. I would write them questions to answer in an effort to encourage them to read and study their Bibles.

I was asked to join a mentor's group because my efforts to help men in this prison were recognized by the staff and prisoners. I accepted the invite and was placed in a co-chair position over a Youth Initiative committee that we had come up with. Troubled and at-risk youth came to visit the prison and meet with us to hear our stories. I always shared my story with them in an effort to help them realize that thinking before taking any action, choice, or decision can prevent them from becoming like me.

I encouraged them to recognize the things that they take for granted could be taken away with one bad choice. God placed it on my heart to put a problem-solving packet together for them that they could take home with them after leaving the prison, so I did. These kids opened up to us about some serious things they were facing and going through. Some cried before us, others admitted that they needed help, and others listened to what we shared and allowed it to change the way that they thought and behaved in the future. The teachers who brought them up to visit us began spreading the word about the impact that we had upon their kids, so many more schools signed up to visit.

I knew that we were having a positive impact on these kids because what they were going through a lot of us who were incarcerated had gone through and knew the outcome of responding to these issues negatively. We shared those outcomes with them and challenged their thinking on how to deal with them in the most productive way. This caused teachers and students to ask questions like, "Why are these guys not given a second chance at life?" That was when the Youth Initiative Committee was cancelled by the prison administrators.

I had been focused on helping men in prison in a more effective way, so I designed a program called, "Building On Experiences." In addition to that, I finished my book, "Establish Your Foundation." Although I could not help the youth in the manner we had been helping them anymore, I knew God was still in control and wanted me to focus my efforts on these works that will benefit people outside of prison as well.

Today, I am able to say that I agree with the Judge, Prosecutor, and the Jury who convicted me of the crime of murder. I was very wrong. The taking of a human life should never be accepted. People going around killing people is not all right. Anyone who does this has to be held accountable. However, it is just as important to help that individual arrive to that conclusion and understand what made them do such a horrible act.

Specialized treatment is what will assist them in arriving to the conclusion that what they did was wrong. When they reach that point, it can lead them to remorse and rehabilitation. God helped me get there. He then gave me a foundation for life by teaching me about HELL, SALVATION, FAITH, HOPE, GRACE, TRUTH, PRAYER, FORGIVENESS, AND LOVE.

These principles have taught me that there are serious consequences for the decision I made because the person I killed belonged to God. I have to answer to Him for that. However, they also taught me that there is deliverance and forgiveness for that, but I needed to do a 180 from the life and thinking that got me there and trust Him to transform me.

These principles are helping me focus on what is truly valuable in my life and reminds me that I have purpose and all the assistance that I need to fulfill God's plan and purpose for my life. They guide me so that I know what decisions and choices to make without harming myself or others. They encourage me to be selfless and respond to all in a manner that God responds to all; love

By the grace of God, I am who I am. I hope that the sharing of these principals helps you as they helped me.

God bless you.

www.ingramcontent.com/pod-product-compliance
Lightning Source LLC
Chambersburg PA
CBHW071853070526
44583CB00016B/1677